Self-Study
of Teaching Practices
PRIMER

PETER LANG
New York • Washington, D.C./Baltimore • Bern
Frankfurt am Main • Berlin • Brussels • Vienna • Oxford

Anastasia P. Samaras
and Anne R. Freese

Self-Study
of Teaching Practices
PRIMER

PETER LANG
New York • Washington, D.C./Baltimore • Bern
Frankfurt am Main • Berlin • Brussels • Vienna • Oxford

Library of Congress Cataloging-in-Publication Data

Samaras, Anastasia P. (Anastasia Pantelides).
Self-study of teaching practices primer /
Anastasia P. Samaras, Anne R. Freese.
p. cm.
Includes bibliographical references.
1. Teachers—Training of. 2. Reflective teaching.
I. Freese, Anne R. II. Title.
LB1707.S263 370.71'1—dc22 2006012713
ISBN 0-8204-6386-8

Bibliographic information published by **Die Deutsche Bibliothek**.
Die Deutsche Bibliothek lists this publication in the "Deutsche
Nationalbibliografie"; detailed bibliographic data is available
on the Internet at http://dnb.ddb.de/.

Cover design by Lisa Barfield

The paper in this book meets the guidelines for permanence and durability
of the Committee on Production Guidelines for Book Longevity
of the Council of Library Resources.

Printed in the United States of America

Table of Contents

1   Introduction 1

2   Foundations of Self-Study of Teaching 23

3   The Nature of Self-Study of Teaching 39

4   Practicing Self-Study of Teaching .55

5   Formal Self-Study of Teaching 81

    References & Resources 113

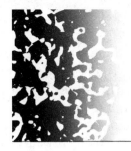

Introduction

Quickwrite

Before we introduce you to self-study, take some time to reflect and then jot down your thinking about self-study. You might consider:

- What do you think of when you hear the phrase "self-study of teaching?"
- Who is involved in self-study?
- Why do you think teachers engage in self-study?
- How do you imagine teachers using self-study?

Jim was a preservice teacher in a two-year master's program that emphasized inquiry, reflection, and collaboration. Like many student teachers, Jim encountered unanticipated frustrations that led to questions about his commitment to teaching. He writes in his journal, "So why bother? I see the end of the program as potentially being just that, the end."

Agonizing over his ineffective classroom management and student teaching performance, he decided to conduct a self-study of his teaching as his master's paper. At the beginning of his paper he wrote: "My

intention in this paper is to come to a better under-
standing of why I have chosen the profession of
teaching. . . . It is my goal to not only put together
my story, as a beginning teacher, but also to reflect
on my own practice in hopes of improving my effectiveness as a teacher."

As Jim systematically analyzed his beliefs about
teaching and his role as a teacher, he wrote, "When
I look back over the past thirteen months I realize
my perspectives on teaching and what it means to
be a teacher have changed. The idyllic philosophies
of the first semester 'arm chair' observer have been
altered significantly after more extensive experiences on the battleground."

We begin this book with a story because self-
study involves our personal stories and our teaching stories that arise out of our own challenges,
frustrations, and dilemmas. Jim is a preservice teacher
who used self-study to discover ways to improve his
teaching and gain insight into his beliefs and practices. He incorporated the tools of self-study to systematically examine issues and concerns in his
classroom. His story and others in this book illustrate how self-study research can be a valuable resource
in our lives as teachers.

We welcome you to the self-study of teaching and
invite you to join us on a reflective, interactive journey into the world of self-study. We will take you
through the background you need to understand
self-study. Then we will provide activities, informal
and formal ones, to engage you in a self-study journey. We have designed "Invitations to Practice" so
that you can try hands-on experiences that will open
up new ways of informing, developing, and rethink-
ing your teaching by studying your practice. More
specifically, in Chapter 1, we present an overview of
self-study of teaching. In Chapter 2, we provide the
history and foundations of self-study of teaching. In
Chapter 3, we describe the nature of self-study of
teaching and outline its key characteristics. In Chapter
4, we explain the self-study of teaching methodology and recommend informal activities for practicing self-study. In Chapter 5, we outline the formal

self-study approach and provide detailed guidelines. We close this final chapter with implications of self-study of teaching. You will also find a glossary at the end of each chapter for easy access and reference to the terminology of self-study and related terms. In the References and Resources section, we have included numerous self-study resources and additional invitations to practice.

We wrote this primer for you with the following five major goals in mind. Our goals are to:

- present the definition, purposes, and an overview of self-study of teaching
- provide the history and foundations of the self-study of teaching
- describe the nature of the self-study of teaching
- share guidelines for practicing the self-study of teaching methodology
- offer field-tested self-study methods with invitations to practice and examples of formal self-study research.

Why Self-Study of Teaching?

We know firsthand that teaching is a challenging profession. In fact, we have observed and participated in many reform movements on the national, state, and local levels which have attempted to improve schooling. We have listened to legislators speak of standards and a silver bullet, while teachers have struggled to implement mandates. We have heard teachers express their feelings of powerlessness and deprofessionalization as decision-making is being done without their input. In all of our years in the profession, the one thing we acknowledge we can change is ourselves. We want to highlight the power and responsibility we have as teachers, and consider the important role we play in the educational system, no matter what that system is. Self-study is key to building **teacher efficacy.** We believe in investing in human capital and especially in students. We believe in you, as teachers, who work hard towards improving education and society.

We also recognize that new teachers face incredible challenges, forcing nearly half of all newly hired

Teacher efficacy

a teacher's belief system and confidence in his or her ability to promote students' learning

teachers to leave the profession within their first five years because of the challenges they encounter (Darling-Hammond, 1997; Colley, 2002; National Center for Educational Statistics, 2005.) According to Ingersoll (2001), teachers leave the profession largely due to inadequate support, a lack of influence, and poor opportunities for professional development. Low-income schools and children in those schools are particularly at risk of teacher turnover (Haberman, 1991.) The self-study of teaching can play an important role in reducing teacher attrition.

We believe that the systematic engagement in the self-study of teaching is a valuable approach for teachers to better understand their teaching and students' learning. It encourages teachers to take charge of their learning and professional development and advance education reform. Self-study is a powerful vehicle that can also help to renew one's passion for teaching. Consequently, self-study advances educational reform efforts in a way that is real and that will make a direct impact in the classroom. Now come along with us to see how self-study relates to your classroom.

Jim's self-study

Let's return for a moment to our story of Jim and see how self-study can provide teachers with the tools for problem solving and give them a sense of empowerment of their teaching. Through his self-study, Jim arrived at some important understandings about himself and about teaching. His self-study resulted in a very basic philosophy that drives his teaching: "What I do should be in the best interest of the student." He stated, "Being too nice is not in the best interest of the students—kids may walk all over you. I am not in the classroom to keep everybody happy."

Jim incorporated teaching strategies aligned with his evolving philosophy. First, he changed his approach from being a "friend to the class," to being "honest, fair and firm." Second, he based his decisions on what is in the best interest of each student.

He stated, "My class consists of twenty-nine individuals. Therefore, providing what is in the best interest of each varies greatly." Third, Jim established a daily community circle which allowed him to hear the unique voices of each student, and build a safe community of learners. Fourth, he formed collaborative groups to foster the community of learners and address the needs of each and every student. Jim's self-study led to transformations in his beliefs and practice. As a result, the classroom management and classroom climate improved, and he developed positive relationships with his students. He learned that becoming a teacher is an evolving process. Most importantly of all, he learned that the students are at the center of the learning community. At the end of his paper, he states, "There is a great deal of value in discovering and realigning one's own philosophy of teaching. Nevertheless, I must remember that teaching is not simply about me, instead, it is about the students who trust me to navigate an entire year of their education."

Jim was a preservice teacher when he became involved in self-study. However, self-study is not only for preservice teachers. Teachers at all points in their careers can conduct self-study. In our next story, we learn about an inservice or practicing teacher who incorporated self-study to help her create a more democratic classroom. Let's look at what she learned through studying her teaching.

Julie's self-study

Julie is a practicing teacher on the edge, exhausted and disappointed about her classroom climate and her students' behavior. She is "burned out" after only two years of teaching. Her main problem is dealing with twenty-seven fourth graders who are constantly calling out and disrupting the flow of her lessons. Julie ponders: "How can I harness classroom talking in a way that will allow for the open flow of ideas while showing concern for the common good and rights of all individuals?" Searching for some solace, she works with a team of teachers and uses the self-study technique of writing about her action research to explore

how her teaching impacts her students' learning. Julie collaborates with other teachers and talks about the changes she will attempt in setting up a democratic classroom, while also looking closely at what she contributes to the conflict at hand.

In her research portfolio Julie writes, "I am learning that the more power you are willing to give to your students, the more respect and responsibility they are willing to give in return." She was successful in creating a more comfortable classroom environment, building trust with her students, and developing a process for self-monitoring using the following multiple strategies: First, Julie conducted student interviews, questionnaires, class surveys, class meetings, and observations to know her students, understand their learning styles and misbehavior. Second, she solicited and implemented students' ideas for agreed upon rules for quiet, listening, class signals, class transitions, and class rules. Third, she developed a series of mini-lessons on social skills geared to help children become more aware of the agreed upon behavior. Fourth, Julie utilized collaborative learning groups where students practiced social skills. Fifth, through a self-study of her teaching practices, she noticed her behavior of talking too much or using too much control. In her journal she reflects:

> Not only am I helping the students to grow and learn about themselves, but I am definitively uncovering details about myself as a teacher and as a person. . . . I really like to take charge of the classroom. . . . It is sometimes hard for me to let them get into groups and run discussions and guide their own learning. . . . This whole process has made me look even harder at the way I run my classroom and the way that students learn.

Julie's story shows us how she has become a more confident, complete teacher as she gains a greater understanding of her students and discovers important insight into her teacher self. These two examples of a preservice and inservice teacher illustrate the value of self-study to their personal and professional development. The examples also high-

light the impact of self-study for classroom improvements.

Why self-study in teacher education programs?

We have witnessed the influence and significance of self-study for enhancing teachers' professional development and life-long learning in the preservice and inservice teacher education programs we directed (Freese, 1999, 2002, 2006; Samaras, 2000, 2002; Samaras & Gismondi, 1998; Samaras, DeMulder, Kayler, Newton, Rigsby, Weller, & Wilcox, 2006; Samaras with Reed, 2000). In each of our programs, students are expected to reflect regularly on their teaching and their students' learning through portfolios, papers, journals, action research projects, evolving philosophies of education, and ongoing semester, yearly, and end of program self-evaluations. Although this is not unlike what may be required of other four-year programs that offer teacher certification and professional development study, our work as self-study teacher educators has encouraged us to offer the self-study of teaching practices to our students.

Why do we do this? You may be curious about us. Who are we? Did we ever teach? What do we do? We'd like to introduce ourselves and briefly share some of our personal experiences in self-study.

Why self-study for us?

We believe in the value of self-study because, like all teachers, we have also faced many challenges in our teaching. We have experienced the benefits of studying our own practice and the power of conducting collaborative self-study. Perhaps you're wondering how we became interested in self-study.

Anastasia

Personal history self-study

the study of the influence of one's culture, context, and history on one's teaching practices

I'm a self-study teacher educator who has been particularly interested in **personal history self-study** or the influence by my culture, context, and history on my teaching practice (Samaras, 2002). You will have a chance to get a closer look at personal history self-

study in Chapter 4. This pull toward a personal history self-study approach was triggered by my studies in Vygotskian (1981) theory and a quest to make his theory practical in teacher education. I began to use a personal history approach with preservice teachers and developed an **education-related life history** assignment which I adapted from the work of Bullough and Gitlin (1995). Finally, I came to appreciate the need for "walking my theory" by not only assigning the work to preservice teachers but by modeling that very practice. I remark: "Because of the openness I ask of my students, I begin with my own snapshots of schooling and perspectives on learning in the hope that they will feel comfortable when they share theirs with our class" (Samaras, Hicks, & Berger, 2004, p. 47). Self-study reminded me that I was always a learner.

This writing is connected to my life as a teacher, teacher educator, and director of two teacher education programs. My teaching career began in 1972 as a junior high school teacher. I taught in mainly public schools over a 16-year period and at various universities for decades. My lived experiences as a social studies teacher and an early childhood teacher impacted my belief in learning with others. My teaching is integrated with my experiences growing up in a second generation immigrant family and my studies in cultural psychology, human development, early childhood education, and teacher education. I apprenticed under superb mentors and learned the value of mediation and self-study with critical friends firsthand.

I have always been interested in how people learn with each other, especially through reflection and dialogue (Samaras, 1995). Regardless of whom I have taught, the young child, the adolescent, or the adult learner, my query has always been the same: What conditions for learning do I create within my own classroom and what difference does that make in my students' learning? This was the beginning of self-study for me although I hadn't named it yet. Over time, my pedagogical knowledge has extended

**Education-related
life history**

a self-study activity that involves reflection on critical or nodal moments in one's learning past that may help to inform one's teaching

from my work with children (Samaras, 1991), to pre-service teachers (Samaras & Gismondi, 1998), to inservice teachers (Samaras, DeMulder, Kayler, Newton, Rigsby, Weller, & Wilcox, 2006), and to faculty (Samaras, Kayler, Rigsby, Weller, & Wilcox, 2006).

Self-study gave me a new lens for professional and program development. It encouraged me to question my theories. It impelled me to rethink and rework the alignment of education methods courses and students' field experiences. It also showed me the value of collaboration and the essentialness of self-study for teachers. This book is an outgrowth of my development as a teacher, a writer, and an artist and the support I received from self-study colleagues in that process.

Along this wonderful journey, I met Anne at a professional conference. Although we live a mainland apart, we have always been connected through our self-study work. We have joyfully collaborated on numerous projects. We have been open and honest with each other. We have talked about the things we have been trying to understand and the things we have wanted to improve in our practice. As the self-study field has continued to develop, we have seen a need to clarify and share it with teachers like you.

Anne

Teaching is my life. Teaching is my passion. I feel very fortunate to be in a profession that allows me to be a lifelong learner and, at the same time, allows me to be a teacher. One aspect of being a lifelong learner involves curiosity and a desire to improve oneself as a teacher. I have discovered over the span of thirty-five years, from my first teaching experience as a sixth-grade teacher in East Los Angeles to my position as a teacher educator, that teaching is a very complex and personal endeavor. Self-study has been a powerful influence in helping me critically examine and inquire into my teaching. Self-study has been a force in helping me improve my teaching and my students' learning.

The work of Schön (1983) has guided my views about the important role reflection and inquiry play

in preservice and inservice teacher education. Dewey's work (1916b) has also influenced my beliefs and practice. He contends that, "Only by wrestling with the conditions of the problem at first hand, seeking and finding [his or her] own way out, does [a person] think" (p. 188). As I began to problematize my work as a teacher educator and engage in self-study, I saw how my beliefs about teaching and learning have changed over the years. I now think about teaching and learning in radically different ways from the way I was taught. Giving lectures, delivering content, administering tests, and assigning grades are not the driving organizational structures of my teaching. Now when I teach, the lives of my students and their lived experiences become an important part of the curriculum. I see it as my responsibility to evoke critical thinking, open-mindedness, problem solving, and reflection by setting up learning events which allow students to question, make connections, draw upon their prior knowledge and experiences, and learn from one another.

In my teaching, I emphasize that one's learning and understanding starts with self, with an awareness of one's beliefs and one's personal theories of learning. I encourage students to reflect on how their past and present experiences have shaped their beliefs and practices. I encourage them to share their personal histories, critical incidents, and philosophies in an intellectually safe community. By reading one another's narratives and personal histories, they broaden their views and open their minds to perspectives and lived experiences other than their own. Through honest dialogue and collaboration, they arrive at a deeper appreciation and understanding of the diverse learning needs and backgrounds they will encounter in their classrooms.

My focus is to create a curriculum which begins with problems, dilemmas, and questions. The curriculum is inquiry-based with the goal of gaining a deeper understanding of teaching and learning by connecting theory with practice. I strive to develop teachers who problematize their teaching and learning, who listen to their students, who learn with

and from their students, and who continually think about and reflect upon their practice. In the same way that I encourage my students to systematically examine their teaching selves, I continuously strive to improve my teaching by engaging in the self-study of my teaching and my students' learning. I do this by encouraging feedback from my students and by researching my teaching. I would not have come to a deeper understanding of the complex, personal nature of teaching and learning, nor would I have reframed my thinking if I had not been involved with self-study research. I am grateful to all of my self-study colleagues, particularly my colleague, Anastasia. They all have been instrumental in helping me grow personally and professionally.

Why self-study for you?

Now that we have talked a bit about why self-study is important to us, you might be asking, but what can self-study do for me? Here are some of the benefits of self-study. Self-study of teaching enables you to:

- better understand yourself, your teaching, and your students' learning
- develop practical knowledge for personal, professional, and classroom improvements
- investigate your own questions situated in your particular context
- improve your teaching and leadership with evidence-based practice
- conduct research with colleagues for grade level, discipline team, and/ or school-wide curriculum improvement

What Is Self-Study of Teaching?

Self-study
teachers' systematic and critical examination of their actions and their context as a path to develop a more consciously driven mode of professional activity

We use the words *self* and *study*, **self-study,** as a component of reflection in which teachers systematically and critically examine their actions and the context of those actions as a way of developing a more consciously driven mode of professional activity (Samaras, 2002). This is in contrast to action based

on habit, tradition, or impulse. Self-study teachers inquire thoughtfully and deliberately into their teaching practice and the assumptions embedded in that practice. In the early years of the self-study movement, self-study scholars struggled to define self-study. Over time, various definitions have emerged from the research experiences of self-study scholars. For example, according to Hamilton and Pinnegar (1998a) "Self-study is the study of one's self, one's actions, one's ideas, as well as the 'not self'" (p. 236). Self-study involves a thoughtful look at texts read, the self as a text, the experiences a teacher had, people they have known, and ideas they have considered. They state:

> As we prepare to do a self-study, we imagine, if you will, that each of us is a text to be reviewed for present and absent ideas and intimately distance our selves from ourselves as if we were a text. As with text, we bring to our reading of self, all of the other textual understandings we have developed over time. No two readings are the same. It is as if we are undertaking a **hermeneutic** study of self. What are we reading? What ideas informed the text? Who informed the text? Why are these ideas and people important to the text? In what ways do these ideas and people miss the point? As we read our 'self-text,' we are looking for the events that influenced our thinking. Why do we have these perspectives? How were we influenced by our ethnicity, gender, and social status? (p. 240)

Hermeneutics
a research process whereby the researcher shifts forward and backward through the data with no predetermined assumptions to allow for the emergence of seemingly unrelated ideas and part-whole relationships

Bullough and Pinnegar (2004) argue that the inclusive nature of self-study and its multiple definitions provoke a continuous and communal conversation about its characteristics. Regardless of the stance, Hamilton and Pinnegar (1998a) conclude "a critical examination of the self's involvement both in aspects of the study and in the phenomenon under study" are central to self-study (p. 240).

Self-study teachers work to articulate knowledge discovered about their practice so their work moves beyond the individual self (Loughran, 2005). The goal of self-study is to investigate questions of practice "that are individually important and also of

broader interest to the teacher education community" (Loughran, 2004, p. 9). With colleagues, self-study teachers collectively question and explore the complexities and possibilities in their teaching, and the interplay of their teaching actions within that exploration.

Teachers often recognize a disparity in what they believe and what they actually do in practice. Whitehead (1989) referred to this gap between one's teaching philosophy and actual practice as a **living contradiction**. Self-study encourages teachers to examine their role and responsibilities to their students. It allows teachers to assess their personal and practical theories in a **situated context** or in a particular setting. This reflective assessment contributes to their development as a person and as a professional and extends the knowledge base of teaching. It also models for students that teachers are also learners. **Pedagogy** requires continuous monitoring throughout one's teaching profession. Self-study teachers continuously examine the perplexities and dilemmas of their teaching practice, while also working to transform the institutional contexts of their work. It is important to note that the self-study of teaching does not have to derive from problematic situations (LaBoskey, 2004b). It can include an exploration of successful teaching and programs practices.

Cochran-Smith and Lytle (2004) discuss self-study as one form of **practitioner inquiry** used by higher education faculty who work in the area of teacher education. They note that self-study often uses biographical, autobiographical, and narrative forms of data collection and analysis. Self-study acknowledges and honors the **postmodern** assumption that the "self" cannot be separated from the research process or in teaching (p. 607). Self-study employs diverse methods and uses primarily **qualitative research** to analyze and represent findings.

Beck, Freese, and Kosnik (2004) describe self-study as an inquiry-oriented approach that is personal, reflective, collaborative, and constructivist. Hence

Living contradiction
a gap between one's teaching philosophy and actual practice

Situated context
the actual place where a phenomenon is studied and where the teaching and learning occurs, e.g., the classroom, school, and/or program

Pedagogy
the art and profession of teaching; the activities and methods of conveying knowledge and skills

Practitioner inquiry
classroom teachers involved in a cycle of questioning, reflecting, and taking action in a situated phenomenon they choose to study

Postmodernism
a worldview that questions a singular truth or governance by established rules to guide one's scholarship

Qualitative research
research that does not rely on quantifiable procedures but instead uses various techniques to probe for depth in the analysis of the object studied

Personal-constructivist-collaborative approach

an inquiry-oriented self-study approach that is personal, reflective, collaborative, and constructivist

they use the term a **personal-constructivist-collaborative approach** to emphasize important components of self-study. Self-study involves a strong personal reference in that it involves study of the self and study by the self. When we identify our own personal focus of inquiry, we feel an ownership of the research and are more motivated to address our dilemmas of practice and gain a deeper understanding of our teaching practice. Self-study is constructivist because it includes elements of ongoing inquiry, respects personal experience, and emphasizes the role of knowledge construction. The collaborative component of self-study acknowledges the important role of the social construction of knowledge.

What Are the Purposes of Self-Study?

There are many purposes of self-study of teaching and those purposes are typically integrated. Cole and Knowles (1998) state that self-study serves purposes that are not mutually exclusive, i.e., first, personal-professional development and, second, a better understanding of teacher education practices, programs, and contexts. Improving one's practice benefits the larger broader purpose of the advancement of knowledge about teaching and the educational system. Thus, the purposes are layered and multifaceted with overlapping objectives and with the key purpose of refining, reframing, and renewing education.

One way to conceptualize the separate, as well as the broader aspects of self-study, is to consider the frame developed by Kosnik, Beck, Freese, and Samaras (2006). They have identified three purposes of self-study conducted by teacher educators who are making a difference in teacher education. The three purposes of self-study for teacher educators are for: first, personal renewal (e.g., Freese, 2006; Feldman, 2006); second, professional renewal (e.g., Ham & Davey, 2006; Mitchell, 2006); and, third, program renewal (e.g., McVarish & Rust, 2006; Kosnik & Beck, 2006). We have adapted the Kosnik, Beck, Freese, and Samaras model for teachers because of its usefulness and comprehensiveness. We outline the major purposes of self-study for teachers as, first, personal growth and development; second, professional growth and development; and, third, classroom and school improvement.

Personal growth and development

Self-study teachers question the underpinnings of their beliefs and practice and the influence of their backgrounds, experiences, and culture on their teaching. In like manner, they begin to acknowledge that each student also has a story connected with his or her own unique upbringing, historical space, and culture. As teachers move through the process of a self-study, they examine and begin to identify who they are as teachers. Self-study can be useful for self-knowing, forming, and reforming a professional identity (Samaras, Hicks, & Berger, 2004). Teachers model continuous learning to students (Freese, 1999). They may question if their actions align with their intentions and beliefs and reflect on ways to improve their practice. Russell (1998) notes that a goal of self-study for teacher educators may very well be the reinvention of learning to teach. On the other hand, self-study teachers may also explore why something they are doing is working well and their role in that process.

Professional growth and development

Self-study enhances professional growth and development for classroom teachers. According to Austin and Senese (2004), self-study serves the purpose of legitimizing the role of classroom teacher as a researcher and a learner, encourages openness for collegial support of classroom events, and recognizes the teacher as central to practice. This ultimately fosters interpersonal teaching and effective learning. When teachers feel a connection between their personal and professional lives, they come to the education enterprise with a wholeness and more complete understanding of schooling.

Self-study allows for a manageable professional inquiry as a teacher struggles to improve one element

of his or her professional practice. Self-study is beneficial because it is context-specific. It focuses on teachers' classrooms, the harsh realities of teaching, and the multiplicity of overlapping dilemmas teachers face daily. It also serves as a platform to develop practical instructional techniques situated in the needed changes identified by the teachers themselves.

It is immediately useful to changes in practice. Teachers are often overwhelmed with their multitasking days. Through self-study, they can select a focus for improving an aspect of their practice. This makes their task manageable, leads to a greater sense of confidence, and encourages them to conduct further self-study generated from their earlier investigations.

Classroom and school improvement

Self-study promotes learning that is open to change in a changing world of teaching. Such change can occur at a classroom or schoolwide level as self-study teachers challenge the status quo of their own teaching practices. Self-study teachers conduct projects for improving their practice and schooling with their colleagues. They invite critical friends into their teaching who provide feedback that is constructive and nonjudgmental. The shared task helps build a collegial problem-solving network for making changes in a classroom, in a grade-level or discipline team, or for schoolwide and districtwide restructuring efforts. The focused support and expertise of colleagues is key to changes in the classroom and school. Similarly, self-study teacher educators question educational practices in their own classrooms and introduce alternative research methods at institutions of higher learning (e.g., Cole, Elijah, & Knowles, 1998; Fitzgerald, Farstad, & Deemer, 2002; Guilfoyle, Hamilton, Pinnegar, & Placier, 1998).

Who Conducts Self-Study?

We encourage you to become a self-study teacher. Historically, self-study scholars have been a dynamic

group of teachers, teacher educators, and administrators committed to studying their practice through self-study in an effort to make their teaching and programs more relevant and effective. Many hold membership in the **Self-Study of Teacher Education Practices (S-STEP) Special Interest Group (SIG)** of the **American Educational Research Association (AERA).** This primer is an extension of the work of that group and was written for you. This primer is for new, as well as seasoned teachers. It is not limited to just one phase of the continuum of teacher development. It is designed to be used as a course textbook or supplemental text for preservice and inservice teachers at the undergraduate or graduate level. Self-study is an essential topic to incorporate in courses dealing with qualitative research, research methodologies, arts-based research, language and culture, professional studies, cultural literacies, or multiple intelligences. Additionally, the primer has relevance for state and county professional development offices which offer professional development workshops for teachers.

The primer is equally applicable to faculty who are interested in improving their teaching practice. We recognize that faculty in teacher education and other fields may not be trained as teachers, and therefore may have a limited repertoire of instructional strategies. The development of their teaching can be additionally impacted by the demands of research and service in the academy. Regardless of discipline, faculty are required by universities to teach, reflect, analyze, and assess their pedagogical development over time, often in teaching portfolios and annual faculty self-evaluations. Self-study of teaching serves to document specific changes made in teaching, curricula, and programs, as well as how the changes were made, and what impact they had on the professor and their students. Universities who promote faculty's teaching development could benefit by providing this primer to new faculty across disciplines because it addresses teaching in general.

Self-study is not limited to teachers and professors. It can involve other practitioners such as administra-

---

Self-Study of Teacher Education Practices (S-STEP) Special Interest Group (SIG)

a dynamic group of teacher educators committed to studying their practice in an effort to make their teaching, curricula, and/or programs more relevant and effective

---

American Educational Research Association (AERA)

a prominent international professional organization with members interested in improving the educational process through scholarly inquiry related to education, dissemination, and practical application of research and results

Self-studyship

the extension of self-study of teaching practice to other practitioners such as administrators, librarians, occupational therapists, psychotherapists, counselors, and other community educators working for social justice and educational reform

tors, librarians, occupational therapists, psychotherapists, counselors, and community educators working for social justice and educational reform (e.g., Allender, 2004; Manke, 2004; Wilcox, Watson, & Paterson, 2004). We call this extension from self-study of teaching practices to other fields as **self-studyship.** As Wilcox, Watson, and Paterson (2002) note, "Self-study allows practitioners to engage in inquiry that contributes to their own capacity for expert and caring professional practice while also contributing to the growth of their professions" (p. 307).

What Is the Self-Study of Teaching Community?

Your self-study work with colleagues will help you to develop a self-study of a teaching community. Many self-study teacher educators have bonded through their collaboration in scholarship and particularly through their **professional membership** and participation in S-STEP. For self-study teacher educators, the self-study of teaching community might be characterized as a **communitas** or a professional community where there are strong feelings of social togetherness and belongingness, often with rituals of practice. The S-STEP SIG has fostered a sense of intellectual safety in a non-competitive and highly supportive culture; much like what we encourage teachers to do in their classrooms. It is a culture that professes that individuals can make a larger impact on advancing teacher education when they work together in a trusting, supportive, and inclusive environment. The SIG practices and models collaboration and learning together. A recent initiative involves the mentorship of SIG members in their publications toward tenure and promotion.

Professional membership

the participation in professional organizations for professional development, networking, and collaboration with colleagues, as well as keeping informed about professional developments

Communitas

a professional community whose members display a strong sense of belonging and social togetherness

Listserv

an interest and subscription based list that uses the e-mail system to send and receive announcements and messages of interest to the members of the group

S-STEP has created a **listserv** which has been useful for conference planning and exchanging papers and ideas. They have also developed a SIG Web page with a community link to members' research (see the References and Resources section). Rituals have emerged at a biannual international conference. For example, presenters at conference sessions receive amusing awards at the opening night of the conference; participants socialize in a common dining area, and they take field trips together. Professional development activities have also taken place in a variety of venues at AERA and other international conferences. Informal and formal discussion groups, research support groups, networking, and visiting each other's universities are common practices in the self-study of teaching community. Membership in S-STEP has also sponsored pre-sessions at AERA and there have been numerous collaborative writing projects such as this book.

We are long-time participants in this "self-study of teaching community" and encourage you to develop a self-study of teaching community with your colleagues. We wish to acknowledge and celebrate more than a decade of work by our self-study colleagues. This primer would not have been possible without their outstanding efforts. We are also grateful to those who have inspired us through their practice and publications about self-study. Their work has informed our writing of the *Invitations of Practice* in Chapter 4. This primer synthesizes much of their research, particularly those who have been leaders in the self-study movement through their involvement in developing and promoting S-STEP.

We are particularly indebted to the editors and chapter authors of the *International Handbook of Self-Study of Teaching and Teacher Education Practices* (Loughran, Hamilton, LaBoskey, & Russell, 2004) whose contributions largely document the self-study movement. We highly recommend this critical resource for further in-depth reading (see Comprehensive References in the References and Resources section). Loughran (2005) notes that self-study by teacher educators displays important parallels to self-study conducted by teachers. We believe this primer will advance that parallel by making the self-study of teaching more accessible and comprehensible to all teachers.

Our work has been supported and extended through our active involvement and leadership in S-STEP and we are deeply indebted to this community.

We have conducted action research and self-study projects with a continuous interrogation and reflection of our teaching practices and underlying assumptions that influence our teaching. Our decade of collaborative scholarship with our self-study colleagues has served as a foundation for writing this primer.

Along with Clare Kosnik, we served as Program Co-chairs and Editors for the Proceedings of the fourth **International Conference on Self-Study of Teacher Education Practices**. These proceedings led to an edited volume of self-study research along with Clive Beck (Kosnik, Beck, Freese, & Samaras, 2006) as well as other writings, (e.g., Samaras, Beck, Freese, & Kosnik, 2005). This biannual, international conference brings together a large group of self-study teacher educators from a wide range of countries around the world. The conference, an outgrowth of the SIG, is also known as **The Castle Conference,** derived from the conference location at Herstmonceux Castle, England. The six biannual conferences held to date at Herstmonceux Castle have attracted participants from both research-intensive and teaching-focused universities (Richards & Russell, 1996; Cole & Finley, 1998; Loughran & Russell, 2000; Kosnik, Freese, & Samaras, 2002; Tidwell, Fitzgerald, Heston, 2004; Fitzgerald, Heston, & Tidwell, 2006).

We write with the hope that you, and teachers everywhere, will embrace the essentialness of studying one's teaching. We worked to catalogue information gleaned from multiple sources and to bring the collection of self-study to a wide audience. We are grateful to the lessons we learned from the many preservice and inservice teachers we have taught and who have also taught us. We welcome your comments as we acknowledge that we are always developing as self-study scholars! Let us begin at the beginning on our self-study journey by exploring how self-study of teaching got started.

International Conference on Self-Study of Teacher Education Practices

a biannual international conference that brings together a large group of self-study teacher educators from a wide range of countries

The Castle Conference

the Castle Conference derived its name from its location at the Herstmonceux Castle in East Sussex, England. Its formal name is the International Conference on Self-Study of Teacher Education Practices

GLOSSARY

American Educational Research Association (AERA)—a prominent international professional organization with members interested in improving the educational process through scholarly inquiry related to education, dissemination, and practical application of research results

Castle Conference—the Castle Conference derived its name from its location at the Herstmonceux Castle in East Sussex, England. The formal name of this biannual conference is The International Conference on Self-Study of Teacher Education Practices

Communitas—a professional community where there are intense feelings of social togetherness and belongingness. It is characterized by rituals of practice

Education-related life history—a self-study activity that involves reflection on critical or nodal moments in one's learning past that may help to inform one's teaching

Hermeneutics—a research process whereby the researcher shifts forward and backward through the data with no predetermined assumptions to allow for the emergence of seemingly unrelated ideas and part-whole relationships

International Conference on Self-Study of Teacher Education Practices—a biannual international conference that brings together a large group of self-study teacher educators from a wide range of countries. The conference is an outgrowth of the S-STEP SIG

Listserv—an e-mailed and interest based discussion list to which one can subscribe in order to receive and send e-mail messages and announcements to a group

Living contradiction—a gap between one's teaching philosophy and actual practice

Pedagogy—the art and profession of teaching; the activities and methods of conveying knowledge and skills

Personal-constructivist-collaborative approach—an inquiry-oriented self-study approach that is personal, reflective, collaborative, and constructivist

Personal history self-study—a study on the influence of one's culture, context, and history on one's teaching practices

Postmodernism—a worldview that questions a singular truth or governance by established rules to guide one's scholarship and being

Practitioner inquiry—classroom teachers involved in a cycle of questioning, reflecting, and taking action in a situated phenomenon they choose to study

Professional membership—people join professional organizations for professional development, to network and collaborate with colleagues, and to acquire and keep abreast of new developments in a particular field. The S-STEP SIG demonstrates the essentialness of that route

Qualitative research—research that does not rely on statistical or quantifiable procedures and instead uses various techniques to probe for depth in the analysis of the object studied

Self-study—a component of reflection in which teachers are asked to systematically and critically examine their actions and the context of those actions as a way of developing a more consciously driven mode of professional activity

Self-Study of Teacher Education Practices Special Interest Group (S-STEP)—a dynamic group of teacher educators committed to studying their practice in an effort to make their teaching, curricula, and/or programs more relevant and effective

Self-studyship—the extension of self-study of teaching practice to other practitioners such as administrators, librarians, occupational therapists, psychotherapists, counselors, and other community educators working for social justice and educational reform

Situated context—the actual place where a phenomenon is studied and where the teaching and learning occurs, e.g., the classroom, school, and/or program

Teacher efficacy—a teacher's belief system and confidence in their ability to promote students' learning

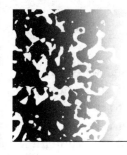

Foundations of Self-Study of Teaching

Quickwrite

How do you think a school of thought and practice develop? What areas of research might have influenced the outgrowth of self-study?

This chapter introduces the historical foundations of the self-study of teaching and the early beginnings of the term self-study. The discussion includes the various research paradigms that have influenced self-study. It also includes a discussion of how self-study has evolved over time. More specifically, the chapter addresses the following three key questions:

- What is the background of self-study?
- What research areas have influenced the outgrowth of self-study?
- How do definitions of self-study inform us about the beginnings, evolution, and formalization of the self-study field?

Background of Self-Study

When searching the Education Resources Information Center (ERIC) database, Loughran (2004)

Descriptor
an object attribute with
binding behavior; a word,
phrase, or characteristic
feature that serves to
describe or identify

found nearly 2000 papers that used self-study as a major **descriptor**. The term self-study comes up in research studies conducted prior to the emergence of the S-STEP SIG and has meant different things depending on how the "self" was defined and interpreted. For example, in the 1960s it appears to draw from three main areas:

- psychology;
- individual learning approaches;
- institutional and program evaluations.

In the area of psychology, self-study has been used "to explore individuals' concept of self" with a focus on "one's personality and the development of self-image" (Loughran, 2004, p. 8). The focus on self was used to explore the psychological aspects of the self (Blumenthal, 1977) as well as the practices of self-disclosure.

Another early usage of the term self-study refers to an individual approach to learning where the learner works independently of a teacher and outside the traditional context of classroom instruction (Glaser, 1966). This approach placed the responsibility of learning on the individual learner through self-paced activities using self-study guides, practice lessons, and self-grading (Loughran, 2004, p. 8). This type of learning approach drew upon Skinner's (1960) behavior modification and accountability research. In this research, the "self" referred to an individual studying alone and taking responsibility for the learning.

Early usage of the self-study term can also be found in the research literature in the area of institutional and program evaluation. Frequently, institutional evaluations were referred to as self-studies. In this context, the "self" generally referred to a university or college and not to an individual. According to Loughran (2004), this type of self-study is most closely connected to our self-study work because it establishes "the expectation that beliefs and practices should be closely aligned and that the self (whether it is a person or program) carries a major responsibility in establishing this alignment" (p. 9).

The historical uses of the term *self-study* show how it has evolved from an individual focus on self and self-image, to an individualized approach to learning, to the evaluation of an institution. The early uses of the terminology of self-study illustrate the diverse understandings of the term prior to the formalization of the self-study movement. However, as we explore the different uses, it is evident that there are similarities between self-study of teaching and the evaluation use of self-study. In addition to the connection to previous uses of the term *self-study,* there are a number of research paradigms that have contributed to the foundations of self-study.

Influential Research Paradigms

Paradigm
a philosophical and theoretical framework of a scientific school or discipline within which theories, laws, and generalizations, and the experiments performed in support of them are formulated

Three major and interconnected educational research **paradigms** have directly influenced the outgrowth, process, and focus of self-study of teaching. The influential research paradigms include, first of all, teacher inquiry, second, action research, and third, reflective practice.

Teacher inquiry

Before the late 1980s, classroom teachers neither viewed themselves as inquirers into their teaching and their students' learning nor did they think about problematizing their experiences or classroom observations to learn more about their students, their context, and their teaching practices. Instead, teachers viewed research as academic-oriented and as something that was done by the experts outside of the classroom. This research was generally conducted by university researchers from various disciplines (Dana & Yendal-Silva, 2003). Teachers' practical and everyday theories of how to improve teaching and learning were neither considered important nor were they made available in teacher education research. Teachers primarily saw their responsibility as implementing what researchers told them was valid in their classrooms.

Questioning one's practice is an integral aspect

of teacher research. This inquiry approach, which emerged in the late 1980s, led to a body of research that focuses on **teacher inquiry** and the teacher as researcher (Duckworth, 1987; Richardson, 1989; Zeichner & Liston, 1996). Prior to the formalization of the area of self-study, a number of teacher educators began to question their teaching and conducted systematic research of their own practice (Cole & Knowles, 1996; LaBoskey, 1994; Russell & Munby, 1992; Zeichner & Liston, 1987; Zeichner, 1996). As teachers and teacher educators inquired into their own practice, they became empowered and better informed about their classrooms, their curricula, and their students' learning.

Teacher inquiry
questioning and conducting research about one's teaching

Reflective practice

Researchers turned to innovative approaches to capture teachers' knowledge and investigate teachers' beliefs and practices. One approach exploring teachers' beliefs and knowledge involved teachers reflecting on their teaching and their students' learning. Researchers found that teachers could examine and problematize their teaching by reflecting on their practice and by becoming **reflective practitioners** (Schön, 1987; Zeichner & Liston, 1996). When teachers critically reflect on their practice, they make sense of the complexities of teaching and participate consciously and creatively in their own growth and development (Schön, 1987; Zeichner, 1999). Munby and Russell (1990) believe that through reflective practice, teachers reinterpret and reframe their experiences from a different perspective. Research in the area of reflection and reflective practice has had a strong influence on self-study. Many self-study researchers, including Russell and Munby (1992), and Loughran (1996) were influenced by Schön's (1983, 1987) and Dewey's (1933) work in reflection. The movement toward developing reflective practitioners has led to a body of research which focuses on the teacher as researcher into his or her own practice (Cochran-Smith & Lytle, 1993; Zeichner & Liston, 1996).

Reflective practitioners
teachers who consciously and creatively examine and problematize their teaching by reflecting on their practice

As teacher educators recognized the value of reflection and inquiry, they began to incorporate a variety of research methods to explore their teacher thinking. By the late 1980s, university researchers of teachers, teaching, and teacher education began to see the possibilities of using the narrative form of inquiry (Connelly & Clandinin, 1990) in their research. They also incorporated biographical and autobiographical forms of inquiry (Russell, 1987; Lawrence-Lightfoot, 1983), and personal histories and oral inquiries (Cochran-Smith & Lytle, 1993). As a result of university researchers adopting these approaches to studying their teaching, it became more acceptable for teacher researchers to study their own practice using these various methodologies of inquiry. These research approaches provided a foundation for teacher researchers to use some of the same methods to systematically study their own practice (Feldman, Paugh, & Mills, 2004).

Action research

Action research

a systematic inquiry conducted by school-based teachers, teacher educators, and community reformers to make informed changes toward curriculum and school improvement in their particular context

In addition to the approaches mentioned above, **action research** has had a direct influence on self-study research. Introduced by Carr and Kemmis (1986), action research involves a systematic approach to problem solving. Teachers and teacher educators became involved in action research (McNiff, 1988; McNiff, Lomax, & Whitehead, 2004; Whitehead, 1989, 1993; Mills, 2000) to examine their teaching and their students' learning as a basis for making changes. Many self-study researchers conducted action research prior to their involvement in self-study.

The shift in the focus of educational research in the late 1980s and early 1990s was characterized by research questions that delved into the complexities of teaching and learning (Loughran, 2005). In addition to this shift in research focus, the role of teachers and teacher educators changed as teachers began to investigate and question their own practice. Research on teaching and schooling became more inclusive, and the knowledge generated about teaching came from the teachers' own questions and won-

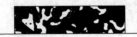

derings, not from the outside experts. Teaching was viewed as highly contextualized, and the research began to focus on the complex and dynamic interactions between the teacher and the students (Dana &Yendal-Silva, 2003). Teachers studying their own teaching spurred research in a number of different areas such as teacher thinking, reflection, and action research. Each of these areas of teacher research has had a strong influence on the growth and interest in self-study.

Self-Study Versus Action Research

"How does self-study differ from action research?" This question was raised at the first Castle Conference and continues to be raised time and again. As mentioned above, action research has had a strong influence on self-study and has been referred to as a "useful tool for self-study" because it provides methods to conduct systematic inquiry into one's teaching practices (Feldman et al., 2004, p. 974). In both action research and self-study, the researcher engages in cycles of research, and systematically collects and analyzes data. Moreover, in both research paradigms, the researcher inquires into problems related to one's practice to improve one's teaching (Feldman et al., 2004). Therefore, both action research and self-study involve, in some cases, similar practices and similar purposes.

It is not surprising that the lines between action research and self-study can become blurred because of their apparent similarities. However, in an attempt to clarify the lines between them, we turn to a thorough analysis of the elements of action research and self-study conducted by Feldman et al. (2004) to explore the differences further. They suggest that one way to differentiate the two research genres is to focus on the relationship between "action" and "research," and "self" and "study." When the accent is on action, there is an assumption that the primary purpose of conducting action research is "to modify or transform one's practice or situation, or those of the community or institution. This means that the collection and analysis of data are used to guide the development of a plan of action or to articulate a critical analysis of the individual and institutional barriers that are shaping their lives" (Feldman et al., 2004, p. 953). They explain that when the accent is on the word "self," then "self" becomes the focus of the study. They argue that this is a "distinguishing characteristic of self-study as a variety of practitioner research" (p. 953).

Another important difference between action research and self-study is that self-study focuses on improvement on both the personal and professional levels. Although self-study may incorporate action research methods, it also incorporates other methodologies, such as narrative inquiry, life history, autobiographies, and biographies.

Another defining feature of self-study is that, although it builds on the personal processes of reflection and inquiry, it takes these processes and makes them open to public critique. Self-study envisions teacher educators, preservice teachers, and inservice teachers learning together as they examine and explore dilemmas of teaching, inquire into questions of practice, and develop and refine their beliefs about teaching and learning. Self-study is not done in isolation, but rather involves students or colleagues working collaboratively to build new understandings through dialogue. Self-study research requires openness and vulnerability since the focus is on the "self." Finally, self-study is designed to lead to the reconceptualization of the role of the teacher.

As we can see, there are a number of factors and research paradigms in the area of teacher research that have influenced self-study. However, there are distinct differences in terms of the relationship of self-study research to other forms of teacher research. Self-study researchers use their experiences as teacher educators as a resource for their research and "problematize their selves in their practice situations" with the goal of reframing their beliefs and/or practice (Feldman, 2002, p. 971). In contrast, action research is more about what the teacher does, and

not so much about who the teacher is.

As we mentioned earlier, teacher educators had written about, discussed, and promoted the use of reflection and action research in their courses in the 1980s, but it took another ten years before teacher educators recognized the value of inquiring, reflecting on, and acting upon their own practice (Korthagen, 1995). In the early 1990s teacher educators began doing what they encouraged preservice and inservice teachers to do: that is, reflect on, inquire into, and study their own practice (Cochran-Smith, 1993; Loughran, 2004; Mills, 2000; Zeichner, 1999). The literature illustrates how the growth and development of self-study has its roots in a number of research areas, and its history reflects how the research interests have become intertwined and evolved from a number of different influences.

Roots of Self-Study to Formalization

One way to understand the current status of self-study is to trace its roots from its inception to the formal field of study. Like any other new area or genre of research, self-study struggled to be recognized as a legitimate field of study. As we trace the development of the language and nature of self-study, we gain insight into how this new research genre continues to refine its language and practices. Thus, we can see how self-study achieved stature as a dynamic, vibrant, legitimate field of research. In the mid-1990s, self-study members began to raise their own questions about the validity of self-study research and how to define the self-study genre. In the next sections, we will explore how the research became more sophisticated and how ground rules were established.

Beginnings of self-study

Self-study researchers have grappled with the notion of "self" for some time. This struggle is evident in Whitehead's (1995) question, "Who is the 'we' in self-study research?" and in Munby's (1996) question, "How and why is self-study research?" Munby also asked, "While I welcome the impact the self-study had on me, I have to question its value for others: why would anyone be interested in what I experienced"? (p. 65). The questions from outside and within the community were valuable in terms of moving the field forward and sharpening its focus. As the self-study field matured, it has made great strides in gaining legitimacy in academia and among educational researchers. What once was considered an alternative, somewhat marginalized area of research, and was characterized as "narcissistic," "self-indulgent," and "egocentric" by some reviewers of research publications, now has acquired a scholarly presence in teacher education (Hamilton et al., 1998).

The field of self-study grew dramatically in a decade's time with the devoted efforts and work of a growing community of self-study researchers. Zeichner (1999) wrote that "the birth of the self-study in teacher education movement around 1990 has been probably the single most significant development ever in the field of teacher education research" (p. 8). A critical development that has thrust the self-study field to the forefront of teacher education research is the voluminous amount of research conducted by self-study researchers. These publications brought much attention and interest to the increasingly popular movement of the self-study of teaching and mark turning points in the coming of age of what we call the **Self-Study School.**

Self-Study School
a popular research movement which began in the early 1990s by teacher educators studying their practice and through member research, presentation, and publication was formalized and came of age a decade later

Evolution of self-study

Although self-study is a relatively young field of research, it has been growing quickly and, at the same time, evolving. There have been numerous writings about self-study for and by teacher educators (e.g., Cole & Knowles, 2000; Hamilton et al., 1998; Kosnik, Beck, Freese, & Samaras, 2006; Loughran & Russell, 1997; Loughran & Russell, 2002; Russell & Korthagen, 1995; Samaras, 2002). While we acknowledge that numerous books have been written about self-study, we will draw upon a few seminal works in the field to help us explore the evolving

definitions of self-study, and see how the field has addressed the emerging issues and concerns. *Reconceptualizing Teaching Practice: Self-Study in Teacher Education* (Hamilton et al., 1998), is an important starting point for understanding self-study because it "explores the philosophical and methodological perspectives of self study" . . . and uses "individual and collaborative case studies . . . to bring these perspectives to life" (Loughran, 2004, p. 10). Hamilton and Pinnegar (1998a) state that the book is designed to "provide evidence that self-study undertaken with rigor . . . will lead to both reconstruction and reconceptualization of teacher education" (pp. 243–244).

Self-study is defined as "the study of one's self, one's actions, one's ideas, as well as the 'not self.' It is autobiographical, historical, cultural, and political and it draws on one's life, but it is more extensive than that. Self-study also involves a thoughtful look at texts read, experiences had, people known, and ideas considered. These are investigated for their connections with and the relationships to practice as a teacher educator" (Hamilton and Pinnegar, 1998a, pp. 236). This broad definition conveys the role of the "self" in self-study and addresses the range of approaches to self-study.

Self-study is described as "qualitative research focused inward" and as a "systematic inquiry into elements of our own practice" Cole and Knowles, 1998, p. 229 and 232). More specifically, self-study utilizes "the characteristic qualitative research tools of observation, interview, and artifact collection, although clearly with different kinds of goals and emphases, it adheres to the same standards of rigor as qualitative research" (Cole & Knowles, 1998, p. 229). Similarities between self-study research and action research begin to surface in this last definition. Self-study is a form of teacher research that focuses on the self and uses qualitative and action research methods. A key difference between action research and self-study, though, lies in the purposes of self-study. Hamilton and Pinnegar (1998b) emphasize the importance of the commitment of the researcher

to examine "one's own practice to bring into action the values that underlie their practice" (p. 1). Self-study researchers continuously examine their practice and are committed to practice what they preach.

Formalization of self-study

The area of self-study became formalized in the early 1990s when it emerged as a recognizable area of research (Loughran, 2004). The first step in developing and formalizing self-study research occurred in a 1992 AERA session on self-study which included the work of some of the self-study leaders, e.g., the "Arizona Group" (Guilfoyle, 1992; Hamilton, 1992; Pinnegar, 1992; Placier, 1992). It was also at this session that Russell (1992) presented his work on "Holding up the mirror: A teacher educator and his students reflect on teaching." These early papers attracted researchers with similar interests. Many of them came from the teacher inquiry, action research, and reflective practitioner research domains. The presenters raised issues and questions about teacher education, such as the "taken for granted assumptions" of teacher education and teacher practices. Some of the other areas of concern included the personal and professional struggles of teachers, the unspoken rules of tenure in the academy, aligning one's beliefs with one's teaching practices, and the nature of learning to teach about teaching (Loughran, 2004; Knowles & Cole, 1991; Trumbull, 1990).

Special Interest Group (SIG)

a SIG provides a forum within AERA for the involvement of individuals drawn together by a common interest in a field of study, teaching, or research

In 1993 the creation of the AERA **Special Interest Group (SIG)**, called the Self Study of Teaching and Teacher Education Practices (S-STEP), was a critical step in formalizing the area of self-study (Hamilton, 1998, p. 235). The establishment of S-STEP marked a significant turning point in creating a community of self-study researchers. Valuable opportunities for professional networking and collaboration among researchers resulted from the SIG's creation, thus contributing to the further development of self-study (Loughran, 2004, p. 16).

Another important influence on the formalization of self-study was the first Castle Conference

held in East Sussex, England in July, 1996. The four-day conference, sponsored by Queen's University in Canada and the Self-Study of Teacher Education and Teacher Education Practices (S-STEP-SIG), drew eighty participants from four continents (Australia, Europe, North America, and South America). The educational researchers in attendance presented papers, created and displayed alternative representations, and explored the philosophy, methodology, and practice of self-study (Hamilton & Pinnegar, 1998c, p. viii).

The Castle Conference has served as an important step forward in bringing researchers together to discuss probing questions, make their knowledge public and open for critique, and collaboratively contribute to the evolving nature of the field. The first Castle Conference was significant in terms of the professional networking and dialoguing that occurred. More importantly, though, it was significant because of the emerging understandings of self-study that grew out of the ongoing discussions and debate, and culminated in the publication of *Reconceptualizing Teaching Practice: Self-Study in Teacher Education* (Hamilton et al., 1998). This book, which brought together the research from the first Castle Conference, provided a strong foundation for the self-study field and was critical in moving the field forward.

Douglas Barnes, a researcher outside the field of self-study, attended the first Castle Conference in 1996. He noted that the definition of self-study was somewhat illusive and difficult to "pin down" as evidenced by the range of self-study papers and research approaches. Barnes conducted a **content analysis** of the conference papers which was helpful in creating a shared understanding about self-study research. In his synthesis of the proceedings, he identified three defining features woven throughout many of the papers. These features are, first of all, openness; second, collaboration; and third, reframing. Barnes noted that these characteristics of self-study research contribute to its distinctiveness, and separate it from action research or teacher

Content analysis

analysis of the manifest and latent content of a body of communicated material through a classification, tabulation, and evaluation of its key symbols and themes in order to ascertain its meaning and probable effect research. He discussed how the self-study researcher must have a disposition that is open to ideas from others, and how collaboration plays a critical role in self-study. He noted that through dialogue and collaboration with other teacher educators and students, the researcher can frame and reframe a problem or situation from different perspectives. Reframing leads one to think about things differently, change one's way of looking at what's going on in classrooms, and ultimately change one's practice in the classroom. He concluded that these characteristics help to define self-study research (Barnes, 1998, p. xii).

The first Castle Conference was followed by five subsequent conferences held in 1998, 2000, 2002, 2004, and 2006 (Richards & Russell, 1996; Cole & Finley, 1998; Loughran & Russell, 2000; Kosnik, Freese, & Samaras, 2002; Tidwell, Fitzgerald, & Heston, 2004; and Fitzgerald, Heston & Tidwell, 2006, respectively). The conferences have continued to bring the self-study community of researchers together to engage in critical discussions and extend the impact of self-study. The conferences have provided a safe space for creating a learning community of self-study researchers who are willing to ask questions, clarify terms, take risks experimenting with innovative approaches, and reexamine and reframe their views about teaching and teacher education practices. The S-STEP SIG formalized the field of self-study research and the Castle Conferences fostered the exploration and discussion about the meaning and value of self-study research. More recently, *Studying Teacher Education,* an international journal of self-study of teacher education practices, has played an important role in contributing to the formalization of the self-study of teaching research. Along with many other publications, *Studying Teacher Education* draws on over a decade of development of the work of self-study teacher educators.

Self-Study as Scholarship

The most definitive and expansive collection of self-study research written to date is contained in

The International Handbook of Self Study of Teaching and Teacher Education Practices (Loughran, Hamilton, LaBoskey, & Russell, 2004). It is a comprehensive compilation of self-study research and practice conducted by researchers from all over the world. "The two-volume handbook contains sixty-one chapter authors from many different countries including the U.S.A., Canada, The Netherlands, Belgium, Iceland, Australia, United Kingdom, and New Zealand. The Handbook is constructed as a major text that fully encompasses the field of self study" (Loughran, 2004, p. ix). These important works were edited by the early leaders in the field and have provided a foundation for the field by exploring the evolving definitions and purposes of self-study. The *Handbook* offers evidence and insight into how the field has matured over the years.

Published eight years after the first Castle Conference, the *Handbook* includes chapters devoted to defining, refining, and extending our understandings of self-study. In the *Handbook* self-study is defined as a research approach that helps the researcher understand "the nature of teaching and teaching about teaching" and ultimately strives to "improve the quality of teacher education" (Loughran, 2004, p. 30). The *Handbook* describes self-study as an important movement for teacher educators which came out of a desire to "combine the best of both worlds; the world of scientific research on education and the world of practice" (Korthagen, 1995; Loughran, 2004, p. 8).

We can see how the questions and provocative discussions that began at the first AERA symposium in 1992 have been raised to a new level of discussion and an enhanced level of scholarship. The publications of *The International Handbook of Self Study of Teaching and Teacher Education Practices* in 2004 and the peer reviewed journal, *Studying Teacher Education: A Journal of Self-Study of Teacher Education Practices* in 2005, are evidence of the dramatic impact self-study research has had in the past decade.

However, as we strive to clarify and provide a

shared understanding of what self-study includes, it is wise to keep in mind the following caveat. "Despite the development, refinement and clarification that has occurred . . . it is clear that the 'one true way,' the template for a self-study method, has not emerged. Rather self-study tends to be methodologically framed through the question/issue/concern under consideration so that it invokes the use of a method(s) that is most appropriate for uncovering the evidence in accord with the purpose/intent of the study" (Loughran et al., 2004, p. 17). Perhaps it is not possible to come up with a "fixed" definition, and perhaps it is not desirable.

Although we may not have a "fixed" definition, self-study scholars continue to research and write about the nature and defining characteristics of self-study. In the next chapter, we deepen our understandings of self-study by exploring these areas of **self-study scholarship**.

Self-study scholarship
the research, presentation, and publication of self-study of teaching practices by researchers devoted to that line of inquiry of practice

GLOSSARY

Action research—a systematic inquiry conducted by school-based teachers, teacher educators, and community reformers to make informed changes toward curriculum and school improvement in their particular context

Content analysis—analysis of the manifest and latent content of a body of communicated material through a classification, tabulation, and evaluation of its key symbols and themes in order to ascertain its meaning and probable effect

Descriptor—an object attribute with binding behavior; a word, phrase, or characteristic feature that serves to describe or identify

Paradigm—a philosophical and theoretical framework of a scientific school or discipline within which theories, laws, and generalizations and the experiments performed in support of them are formulated; an interrelated set of assumptions about how things are and must be (see Kuhn, 1970)

Reflective practitioner—teachers who consciously and creatively examine and problematize their teaching by reflecting on their practice

Self-study scholarship—the research, presentation, and publication of self-study of teaching practices by researchers devoted

to that line of inquiry of practice

Self-Study School—a popular research movement which began in the early 1990s by teacher educators studying their practice and through member research, presentation, and publication was formalized and came of age a decade later

Special Interest Group (SIG)—A SIG provides a forum within AERA for the involvement of individuals drawn together by a common interest in a field of study, teaching, or research

Teacher inquiry—questioning and conducting research about one's teaching

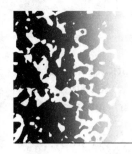

The Nature of Self-Study of Teaching

Quickwrite

We often hear about process versus product in the field of education. How do you think that applies to self-study? Take some time to reflect and write, draw, or discuss what you think we mean when we refer to the self-study process.

Now that you have learned about the foundations of self-study, you might be wondering, "Okay now I see how it started, but what do we mean when we talk about the nature of self-study?" "What are its characteristics?" Let's turn to that next. This chapter addresses three key questions about the nature of self-study:

- What are the characteristics of self-study?
- How is self-study a process for professional development?
- What is the paradoxical nature of self-study?

The literature on self-study reveals that self-study scholars have thought deeply about what self-study is, what it involves, and what distinguishes it from

other research areas. This articulation has included much discussion and delineation by self-study scholars. They have written about its unique characteristics as a research methodology which in turn contributed to the formalization of self-study. Some self-study scholars have described self-study as an examination of the personal within a specific context, while others have focused their discussion about its interpersonal nature.

In an effort to be concise and direct, we collected and examined the work of self-study scholars who speak about the characteristics of self-study. We synthesized the many separate features into five central characteristics listed below:

1   self-study is situated inquiry;
2   self-study is process;
3   self-study is knowledge;
4   self-study is multiple;
5   self-study is paradoxical.

When we first became interested in self-study, this last characteristic was confusing for us, i.e., self-study is embedded with paradoxes. Its dualistic nature may also seem contradictory or confusing at times. So we decided to articulate our insights about the characteristics and paradoxes of self-study in this primer.

Central Characteristics of Self-Study

Characteristic 1—Self-study is situated inquiry

Situated inquiry
inquiry is driven from practitioners' own questions situated in their particular context

Self-study is **situated inquiry**. That means it begins with your inquiry and is driven from your questions situated in your particular context. It is a self-initiated inquiry of practice and draws from the authority of a practitioner's experience (Pinnegar, 1998). Motivation is built into the process of self-study because you are asking your own question(s) that impact you and your classroom. You are vested and involved because you are the direct recipient of the results. The change is personal, immediate, and compelling because it is connected to your learning and

that of your students.

Self-study provides relevance and utility to practitioners particularly because the inquiry is contextually bound. Research is grounded in the living issues of practice and it incorporates the persons in their context or setting. Drawing upon students' questions, interests, and puzzlements with experiential learning is central to their meaning making (Caine & Caine, 1994; Dewey, 1938; Knowles, 1970). Similarly, inquiry generated from teachers' interests and school-based issues is essential to their professional development (Hawley & Valli, 1999).

Knowledge generated by practitioners' inquiries, as opposed to those of outside researchers, has immediate utility to the practitioner's context (Cochran-Smith & Lytle, 1993, 2004). Self-study authenticates the teacher's role as a researcher. This key characteristic of personal inquiry is central to professional practice and educational reform (Wilcox, Watson, & Paterson, 2004). Inquiring into one's own practice leads to a clearer understanding of the complexities, dilemmas, and contradictions of teaching and learning for students and teachers alike (Loughran, 2004; Whitehead, 2004). Hamilton & Pinnegar (1998a) explain that "The multilayered, critically-imbued, reality-ladened world is the text of the self-study scholars . . ." (p. 235).

Self-study positions the teacher as an inquirer and learner. Indeed Clarke and Erickson (2004) note teaching and learning are keenly integrated. They argue that inquiry is the cornerstone of professional, as opposed to technical, practice. Self-study as a type of practitioner inquiry enables teachers to ask themselves the difficult questions where there are no easy answers, only choices (Senese, 2002; Tidwell, 2002). They acknowledge, reflect, and act upon the dissonance they uncover between their beliefs and practice and openly share the dilemmas with colleagues. Self-study scholars inquire into the **epistemological** underpinnings of their assumptions about knowledge and reality (LaBoskey, 2004b). They examine the past and present to inform future possibilities. The

---

Epistemology

Epistemology deals with how people come to know, understand, and develop a worldview. It is the study or a theory of the nature and grounds of knowledge especially with reference to its limits and validity. Self-study scholars question their assumptions of practice while viewing themselves as knowers who socially construct knowledge

Ontology

Ontology is a branch of metaphysics concerned with the nature and relations of being

inquiry is functional, historical, **ontological**, and moral in nature (Bullough & Pinnegar, 2004). Self-study demands an honest and moral stance. Inherently, teaching includes an obligation to improve a learning situation for oneself and for others through the inquiry (Bullough & Pinnegar, 2001).

Using reflection, practitioners encounter what Schwab (1973) calls the commonplaces of teaching, i.e., every teaching situation includes, first, the teacher, second, the student, third, the subject matter, and fourth, the context. Clarke and Erickson (2004) add self-study as a fifth commonplace or the "some how" or way to study one's practice. For example, Samaras (2002) extends Schwab's model of reflection to incorporate her self-study inquiry. She demonstrates the "some how" of her teaching, i.e., why and how she integrates Vygotskian principles in her teaching and program restructuring. Lev Vygotsky, a renowned Russian developmental psychologist, believed that humans are significantly influenced by the social and historical context which mediates their experience. They learn in the historical and cultural contexts of their times. Social and cultural influences shape development, and individuals also shape the historical period in which they live. An inquiry on that influence may help teachers consider the implications of culture on schooling.

Characteristic 2—Self-study is process

Self-study is a process that gives you permission to change your teaching philosophy without incurring guilt over past practices and beliefs. It changes the culture of blame and guilt and takes it to the frame of investigating and reframing practice over time. As teachers we know that change may cause feelings of discomfort, albeit not necessarily pleasant, yet essential in developing new perspectives and understandings (Berry, 2004). The self-study journey is not necessarily linear. How you decide to use it depends a great deal on the direction you choose to take.

Self-study is a systematic and sustained process, where inquiry is longitudinal in nature. Hoban (2004) asserts the need to document the processes of the self-study inquiry, i.e., representing, editing, accessing, analyzing, retrieving, and sharing data. He utilizes technology to that end in his self-study research. Self-study is a change journey in a hermeneutic spiral of questioning, discovery, challenge, hope, and change. We'll give you examples of that in the next chapter.

Although self-study requires immediate action, the results create extended opportunities for self-study and altered foci (Loughran & Northfield, 1998). Through self-study, teachers can implement a manageable inquiry and see the immediate results knowing that there are possibilities for further change. Teachers can also repeat the self-study process multiple times to compare the results. There may be scenarios where the teacher reads about others doing self-study and what they experienced.

Self-study professes modeling, but not molding or a grand theory. There is no end to studying one's practice. Teachers do not have final answers to the issues they face, but they should be able to follow new developments and articulate and pose their own questions (Austin & Senese, 2004). The aim of self-study is to understand, not to assert a particular claim or final knowing (Pinnegar, 1998). Teachers become knowledgeable and "come to know" their teaching (LaBoskey, 2004b). Knowledge is built over time and can change as new information is gained. The improvement-aimed work conducted by self-study teachers is designed to enrich the scope and breadth of one's ongoing understanding about practice and educational programs.

Characteristic 3—Self-study is knowledge

Self-study provides fertile ground for investigating and developing your knowledge about teaching with evidence that is immediate and personal. It can support and inform program reform and policy decisions thereby contributing broadly to the

knowledge base of teaching. We find that the inquiries of self-study teachers extend the knowledge base of teaching in three unique, yet highly integrated domains, first, the personal, second, the professional, and third, the classroom, school, program, and/or institution (Kosnik, Beck, Freese, & Samaras, 2006).

On a personal level, self-study of teaching builds self-knowledge. Kincheloe (1991) notes that there is no knowledge without the knower. The perspective of the researcher must be granted the same seriousness and attention as the research design. Self-study scholars question their practice and arrive at new understandings of their teaching. They create new knowledge as they reframe their practice through their questioning of the assumptions of their practices. Self-study embraces Dewey's belief that "no thought, no idea, can possibly be conveyed as an idea from one person to another . . . Only by wrestling with the conditions of the problem at first hand, seeking and finding [his or her] own way out, does [a person] think" (Dewey, 1916a, p. 188). Schön (1983) made a parallel point about professional learning, arguing that practitioners must generate their own professional knowledge in the context of practice. They cannot take the "expert" knowledge developed in universities and simply apply it as mere technicians.

Self-study is based on personal experience. Systematically portraying that investigation works to validate self-study as research and promote the personal experience as a source of new knowledge (Loughran & Northfield, 1998). It gives teachers an opportunity to consider the role of self in teaching or the "teacher self" (Allender, 2001). It embraces the entire person and looks at the broad landscape of teacher knowledge which includes the emotional, political, and moral dimensions of teaching (Kelchtermans & Hamilton, 2004; Trumbull, 2004). The positionality of the researcher is integrated, not objectified, from a research study grounded in the lived experiences of one's personal practice.

On a professional level, self-study extends scholarship, ownership, and creativity into the hands of teachers as professionals. Teachers openly share their teaching struggles, their accomplishments, and their challenges. Their work illuminates and guides others in understanding that teaching is an artistry and a science. As artists, teachers experiment and research using creative and nontraditional methods, particularly arts-based methods (see the Invitations to Practice section in Chapter 4). Self-study teachers use multiple ways of learning and researching. As scientists, self-study teachers question a particular phenomenon in a particular context. They document, analyze, and articulate their findings to a scholarly community for their peer review. Self-study scholars have called for high quality and standards with a delivery of evidence (Bullough & Pinnegar, 2001; Hoban, 2004; Knowles & Cole with Presswood, 1994; LaBoskey, 2004b; Trumbull, 2004; Whitehead, 2004). Increasingly, self-study scholars have responded to this call which has contributed to its formalization.

On a program and institutional level, teachers seek to understand their role in improving programs and schools and work to make significant changes in education. Self-study scholars' critical examination of their practices contributes to the knowledge and understanding of teacher education and the education reform movement (Zeichner, 1999). Self-study teachers question the status quo of teaching, schools, the academy, and traditional research methodologies (Hamilton, 2004). Although complex, self-study supports the development of knowledge of the individual, the professional, and the program. As Berry (2004), states . . ."At the same time, it becomes a powerful and significant approach to researching teacher education" (p. 1304).

Self-study research yields insights for program development involving school-university partnerships (e.g., Kosnik, 1998), for departmental communication (e.g., Upitis & Russell, 1998) and for institutional support toward teacher reform (e.g., Cole, Elijah, & Knowles, 1998). The improvement provides evidence for change and reframing for pro-

gram and/or institutional purposes. According to LaBoskey (2004b) that improvement can include change that is political. It can work toward social justice. Self-study research is humane, moral, and ethical. Those components extend the knowledge base of effective teaching and schooling practices.

Characteristic 4—Self-study is multiple

Self-study is multiple and multifaceted. By that we mean self-study teachers can practice self-study using different theories, various research methods, and with numerous purposes. We'll talk more about self-study as a methodology and its methods in the next chapter. For now, let's consider how it is multiple in, first of all, theoretical stance, second, research method, and, third, purpose.

Multiple in theoretical stance

Each discipline has a set of theoretical principles which have historically guided their profession. For example, in teacher preparation, students are introduced to the theories of teaching and learning. Those theories are often the basis for class discussions, assignments, and examination. As teacher education students begin their school observations and intermittent teaching, they are asked to notice those principles in practice. Bullough and Pinnegar (2001) bring attention to the need that practice brings meaning to theory and state, "Only when a theory can be seen to have efficacy in a practical arena will that theory have a life" (p. 15). Theory is translated through the personal. However, the study does not focus on the self alone but on one's role in affecting practice.

Self-study scholars may uncover their early attraction toward a particular theory or their developing practical theory (Samaras, 2002), but it is important to note that self-study scholarship scholars come from multiple theoretical points of view. Although self-study scholars may have a preference towards particular theories (e.g., Dewey, 1916a, 1938; Bourdieu, 1990; Fosnot, 1989; Schön, 1993; or Vygotsky, 1978),

self-study research does not include a particular theoretical stance.

Self-study is often noted as rooted in a postmodern theoretical perspective because of its non-linear and unpredictable nature (Wilcox, Watson, & Paterson, 2004). A modernist researcher assumes knowledge as a given prior to the act of research. A postmodern researcher understands knowledge production as a **cultural production**. More specifically, the researcher takes a reflective and analytical stance and seek to identify the cultural, interpretive, and ideological basis built into his/her conceptions of knowledge. This is particularly important for education students and teachers as they sort through their biases that impact their interactions and perceptions of others in their teaching.

Cultural production
the cultural, interpretive, and ideological basis built into one's generation and conception of knowledge

Self-study examines the practical and brings the theoretical underpinnings of one's work to the forefront. As self-study draws from the practical, the **tacit theory** may not be explicit to the reader but rather unfolds as the researcher uncovers his/her theoretical perspective (Clarke & Erickson, 2004). A **feminist methodology** has also been frequently employed by self-study scholars, (e.g., Coia & Taylor, 2004; Mitchell & Weber, 1999; Samaras, 2002). Feminists question how their identity and gender interplay in their construction of reality (Belenky, Clinchy, Goldberger, & Tarule, 1986; Britzman, 1991).

Tacit theory
a theory that is implicit or indicated but not actually expressed

Feminist methodology
a type of research employed by researchers who question how their identity and gender interplay in their construction of reality

Multiple in research method

Secondly, self-study scholars conduct practitioner research with multiple and diverse qualitative methods (Samaras, Hicks, & Berger, 2004). Those methods are derived from comparable methodologies and are well grounded in one's moral, ethical, and political principles (LaBoskey, 2004a). Autobiographical and personal history self-study, narratives, **memory work**, and multiple artistic modes such as visual representations, theater, drama, and poetry are some of the methods that self-study scholars have employed (Lighthall, 2004; LaBoskey, 2004b). Regardless of theory or method, research

Memory work
a self-study method used to represent autobiographical inquiry with critical and reflective revisiting

yields data and requires analysis of an issue in a particular time and context (see Chapter 4).

Multiple in purpose

Third, self-study is multi-purposed with the common intent in leading to valuable outcomes for the teacher and the students. Self-study serves individuals and programs in different ways. It has been used by teacher educators, by classroom teachers, counselors, and administrators. Each self-study has a particular and unique focus for the self-study scholar. The varied theoretical stances, methods, and purposes of self-study have enriched the self-study community by providing multiple perspectives on what is knowledge and how one seeks to understand one's own practice through self-study research.

Characteristic 5—Self-study is paradoxical

When we were reviewing the nature of self-study, a series of interesting paradoxes presented themselves to us. We discuss three inherently dualistic paradoxes that captured our attention. We cite research that supports our thesis that self-study is paradoxical.

Paradox 1. Self-study is individual and collective

The individual perspective may be a "significant paradox" in self-study terminology (Loughran & Northfield, 1998). The term *self-study* suggests that the individual is the focus of the study. What it does not reveal is that the work of self-study is a collective task as well (Elijah, 2004).

Self-study respects the notion that we teach who we are and who we are becoming as professionals. Teachers ask themselves questions such as, "How did I arrive at the assumptions, dispositions, and attitudes I have about teaching and learning?" "What are the implications of those beliefs to students' learning?" "How do my culture and history shape my development as a teacher?" Like teachers, students also have been shaped by their cultures and are shaping their world (Vygotsky, 1981). As self-study researchers examine who they are as teachers, how they arrived at a place, and how they are changing, knowledge is created about themselves and their interactions with students.

Bullough and Pinnegar (2004) explain that self-study rests on the premise of "learning as a change in behavior" (p. 320). Learning might be generated from examining and aligning one's beliefs to practice (Guilfoyle, Hamilton, Pinnegar, & Glacier, 1998). It may arise as one seeks to understand issues of race, ethnicity, and gender (e.g., Brown, 2002) or one's positionality and relationship to students (e.g., Clift et al., 2006). Nonetheless, a fundamental requirement of self-study is that it is collective (Ham & Kane, 2004; Loughran, 2004).

The process of self-study is a practice of self-directed professional development and it has a self-monitoring nature. Critical friends, with alternative views, improve the process (Bass, Anderson-Patton, & Allender, 2002; Wilcox, Watson, & Paterson (2004). Trusted colleagues ask the self-study teacher for clarification and work to validate the experiences and/or offer alternatives (Barnes, 1998). As self-study teachers make their research known to others, they share a commitment to better understanding their practice. Self-study requires a commitment to outside interpretations and a willingness to review one's existing frames.

Furthermore, self-study work can be individual self-studies or collective ones. Audience is central to both. Bullough and Pinnegar (2001), LaBoskey (2004a), Loughran (2004), and Whitehead (2004) argue that self-study scholars must have a deep commitment to checking data and interpretations with colleagues to broaden possibilities and challenge perspectives. This in turn increases the credibility and **self-study validity**. Validity in conventional research involves empirical evidence, generalizability, and professional critique. In self-study, multiple perspectives, including that of the researcher, are a strong validator of the findings (Ham & Kane, 2004; Loughran & Northfield, 1998). Ham and Kane (2004) clarify that the self is the instrument and the

Self-study validity

multiple perspectives gained from critical friends in relation to one's own beliefs and actions are necessary to validate one's self-study efforts

self-study teacher is not only the person doing the seeing; he or she is also the person being seen.

Paradox 2. Self-study is personal and interpersonal

Self-study is personal because it is constructed from knowledge generated from a teacher's everyday practices and practical theories. Hamilton and Pinnegar (1998a) state that in addition to personal theorizing, "knowing and understanding the self is an essential aspect for generating change and developing new knowledge" (p. 241). In the words of Ham and Kane (2004) " . . . the study of teaching is not purely the study of the personal, but of the personal within the professional . . . It is inherently, therefore, a study of that which binds the particular to the collective, a study of that which assumes a 'we,' a collegial society or culture of others who spend much of their waking hours being what I am, doing what I do" (p. 116).

Self-study acknowledges that teachers are willing to examine their own behavior and think about the implications of their actions for their students. It expresses both a risk and a commitment for teachers to change themselves. Bass, Anderson-Patton, and Allender (2002) describe self-study as a creative, collective, and cyclical process with the change in practice encompassing a change in self.

Self-study is also interpersonal, interactive, and collaborative. According to Vygotsky (1978), cognition is always **socially mediated**, or influenced by others in social interaction and especially through language. Learning, thinking, and knowing arise through collaboration and reappropriating feedback from others which aligns with **sociocultural theory**. Smith (1998) notes that personal meanings arise from activities that are valued by and with other members of a culture. Drawing upon multiple sources of assistance provides more opportunities within the multiple **zones of proximal development.** In this manner, individuals can better reach new understandings through others. Another way to think about it is that knowledge is distributed and con-

Socially mediated
cognition is always socially mediated or influenced by others in social interaction. Thinking begins on an interpersonal or social plane before it can be internalized as intrapersonal knowledge

Sociocultural theory
a theory based on the belief that humans are significantly influenced by the social and historical context that mediates their experiences and that individuals shape the historical period in which they live

Zone of proximal development
a Vygotskian principle of learning

structed with various areas of expertise in a collaborative enterprise, in situated practice (Brown, Collins, & Duguid, 1989; Brown, 2002; Bruner, 1990), or in **learning zones** (Samaras, 2002; Samaras et al., 2006).

Learning zones
organic and diverse communities of expertise where learners co-mediate, negotiate, and socially construct an understanding of a shared task

A self-study community encourages the sharing of new insights, both positive and negative. The knowledge building occurs through knowledge sharing and knowledge creation in a self-study community. It is as if the community "leads" (Vygotsky, 1978) or "completes" (Newman & Holzman, 1993) development. Community as audience is central to self-study. Kosnik, Beck, & Freese (2004) state that an inclusive and equitable self-study of teaching community fosters personal and professional growth. LaBoskey (2004a) affirms the need for a supportive and interactive community in the knowledge building process.

Collaboration does not mean harmony. The interaction may cause the individual to question his/her position or those of others as they develop new understandings. Elijah (2004) speaks of the multivoiced texts as including the voice(s) of the writer and the voice of the reader and with meaning negotiated. Beyond the cognitive level, self-study scholars also have the emotional support of self-study colleagues who are invested in improving learning through self-study.

Paradox 3. Self-study is private and public

Self-study involves a sincere concern and one that has been private. It may begin with reflective journal writing (Russell, 2006), a personal diary (Mitchell 2006), and/or kept letters of a trusted colleague (Knowles & Cole, 1994). The dilemmas are private, but when they are written down and eventually published, they become public. Samaras (1998) states, "There is a definite disrobing in publishing self-study where one is immediately exposed to public view" (p. 55). Nonetheless, it is in the very act of recognizing and sharing the dissonance that allows teachers to work toward change (Russell, 2002).

Reflection is integral to self-study and allows one to think, reframe, and act on practice. Loughran

and Northfield (1998) explain that "self-study takes these processes and makes them public, thus leading to another series of processes that need to reside outside the individual" (p. 15). Self-study scholars believe there is a commitment to make self-study public (Bullough & Pinnegar, 2004) so that the work may be useful to others. It becomes collective knowledge when it is public and shared with an audience. The audience is critical in shaping self-study reports (Bullough & Pinnegar, 2004; Loughran & Northfield, 1998). The need for critical friends and public credibility in self-study demands a transparency and openness (Barnes, 1998; Clarke & Erickson, 2004). The public deliberation formalizes the self-study work (LaBoskey, 2004a).

Self-study scholars speak of "walking our talk" and "practicing what we preach" (Guilfoyle, Hamilton, Pinnegar, & Placier, 1998). The public nature of self-study often involves an activist stance where the private moves to the public for morally, ethically, or politically based educational reform (LaBoskey, 2004a). Hamilton & Pinnegar (2000) stress the need for teacher educators to systematically collect data and to study their teaching practice, thus demonstrating their "trustworthiness" to their students. One essential aspect of self-study involves being honest and taking risks in the inquiry and reflection of one's beliefs and practice. Because this approach involves a certain level of vulnerability, it is important that the learning community is an intellectually safe context. A self-initiated, honest, and public stance about one's practice can lead to improvements in students' learning and one's own learning.

Organic and Ongoing

The five central characteristics capture many of the separate features of self-study that self-study scholars have identified. In sum, self-study is:

1 situated inquiry;
2 process;
3 knowledge;

4 multiple;

5 paradoxical.

The three paradoxes highlight the complexity, the uniqueness, and the potential of self-study. Paradoxically, self-study is, first, individual and collective; second, personal and interpersonal; and third, private and public.

Its organic nature invites self-study scholars to continue to explore, discuss, and contribute to the conversation about the characteristics they identify through their research-based practice. The ongoing process-oriented nature of self-study reminds us that as the field continues to develop, its characteristics will continue to be defined, refined, and extended. Now that we have discussed the foundations and nature of study, in the next chapter we provide the guidelines for conducting self-study with invitations to practice it.

GLOSSARY

Cultural production—the cultural, interpretive, and ideological basis built into one's generation and conception of knowledge

Epistemology—Epistemology deals with how people come to know, understand, and develop a worldview. It is the study or a theory of the nature and grounds of knowledge especially with reference to its limits and validity. Self-study scholars question their assumptions of practice while viewing themselves as knowers who socially construct knowledge

Feminist methodology—a type of research employed by researchers who question how their identity and gender interplay in their construction of reality

Learning Zones—Learning zones are organic and diverse communities of expertise where learners co-mediate, negotiate, and socially construct an understanding of a shared task

Memory work—A self-study method used to represent autobiographical inquiry with critical and reflective revisiting

Ontology—Ontology is a branch of metaphysics concerned with the nature and relations of being

Self-study validity—multiple perspectives gained from critical friends in relation to one's own beliefs and actions are necessary to validate one's self-study

Situated inquiry—inquiry is driven from practitioners' own questions situated in their particular context

Socially mediated—according to Vygotsky (1978), cognition is always socially mediated or influenced by others in social interaction. Thinking begins on an interpersonal or social plane before it can be internalized as intrapersonal knowledge

Sociocultural theory—a theory developed by Lev Vygotsky, a renowned Russian developmental psychologist, who believed that humans are significantly influenced by the social and historical contexts that mediate their experiences. Social and cultural influences shape development, and individuals also shape the historical period in which they live

Tacit theories—theories that are implied or indicated but not actually expressed

Zone of Proximal Development (ZPD)—a Vygotskian principle of learning where "the distance between the actual developmental level as determined by independent problem solving and the level of potential development as determined through problem solving under adult guidance or in collaboration with more capable peers" (Vygotsky, 1978, p. 85)

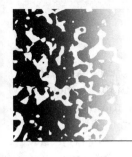

CHAPTER FOUR

Practicing Self-Study of Teaching

Quickwrite

Brainstorm the issues you might like to consider for a self-study project for your personal or professional growth and development, and/or classroom or school-wide level improvement. Jot down those ideas now.

In previous chapters we mentioned that a fundamental, underlying question of self-study research is "How can I improve what I am doing?" In this chapter we explore how we can answer this question by practicing and applying the self-study methodology. We discuss how self-study involves systematically exploring the tensions of practice and the dilemmas of teaching. Furthermore, we see how self-study allows us to gain meaningful insights into our teaching and our students' learning through situated inquiry into our practice. The chapter focuses on developing and deepening our understandings of the methodology of self-study, as well as providing opportunities to practice various methods of self-study research. We do this by including invitations to practice self-study.

The invitations to practice include examples of field-tested self-study teaching activities which illustrate the utility of the self-study methodology for teachers and their students. Loughran (2004) reminds us that the self-study of teaching does not offer a bag of tricks to enact or that one can "fix" teaching. Conversely, Knowles, Cole, & Presswood (1994) emphasize that due to the complexities, difficulties, and problematic nature of teaching, there is no recipe for a "best" teacher or one "right" way of teaching. Therefore, we see self-study of teaching as the opportunity to explore the challenges of teaching and find solutions to those challenges. The self-study teaching activities are offered as examples and not as step fashioned formulas or blueprints. We want to re-emphasize that self-study is not a "recipe" or a "procedure," rather it is a valuable methodology (Bullough & Pinnegar, 2004) for teachers. The suggested invitations help us move from the theory of self-study to providing ways to apply it in our practice. This chapter addresses four key questions about practicing self-study of teaching:

- What is the methodology of self-study?
- What are the methods of self-study of teaching?
- What are the approaches of self-study?
- How does informal self-study look in practice?

Methodology of Self-Study

In this section we introduce the self-study of teaching as a methodology. We clarify the meaning of the term, self-study "methodology" and discuss how self-study "methodology" differs from "methods." We begin by defining some key terms to gain an understanding of the methodology of self-study and the methods used to conduct a self-study. There is often confusion about the terms *methodology* and *methods*. In fact, it is not unusual to see the words used interchangeably.

We use the term self-study **methodology** to refer to a stance toward the research question that can employ many methods (LaBoskey, 2004b). The methodology was developed by self-study teacher educators to enhance their teaching practice and provide

Methodology

a body of practices, procedures, and guidelines used by those who work in a discipline or engage in an inquiry

evidence within their context to understand their practice (Hamilton & Pinnegar, 1998c). Teachers take informed action on what is learned through situated inquiry and dialogue with critical friends.

Self-Study Dispositions

Before we move on, we want to take a moment and trace back over some of the key concepts we discussed in the previous chapters. The overlap is purposeful so that we can bridge the interconnections of the foundations, nature, and methodology of self-study. We bring your attention to particular characteristics as they relate to the methodology requirements.

Reflection

In Chapter 2, we talked about how the Self-Study School grew partially from the work of scholars working in the areas of teacher inquiry, reflection, and action research. We believe that when you, as a learner, are personally engaged and reflective in your self-study, you will gain an increased understanding of what self-study entails and gain an appreciation of the benefits of self-study. As teachers, we engage in reflection on a daily basis. We reflect on what went well, what did not, and what changes we can make to improve our lessons. As teacher educators, we encourage our students to reflect on and evaluate their lessons, because we view reflection as a critical component of teachers' professional growth. Reflection can be viewed as a stepping stone to inquiring into our practice. In addition, we view reflection and inquiry as stepping stones to self-study.

In Chapter 2, we also talked about how self-study differs from reflection and action research. In Chapter 3, we explained how sharing self-study with colleagues makes your work public and accessible, and enhanced as a result of multiple perspectives.

Collaboration

Although reflection can be done individually, collaborative reflection is essential to the self-study process (Loughran, 2004). Collaboration helps us

move beyond our own personal views by hearing other perspectives. It provides opportunities for support, new insights into our work, as well as different perspectives. When we engage in individually studying or reflecting on our practice, there is a tendency to be too narrow. Collaboration encourages reflection beyond the self, and includes collective reflection on the issues. This collaborative reflection leads to different perspectives, probing questions, opportunities for clarification, and alternative explanations. These new insights and questions can trigger alternative perspectives and lead to further questions. Collaboration also contributes to a validation of the findings because the analysis extends beyond one's personal views, thus addressing potential biases.

Openness

We have mentioned how collaboration plays a valuable role in self-study. Yet we acknowledge that sharing our dilemmas and concerns with others can be a bit threatening and scary. In our work with pre-service and inservice teachers, we have seen the tendency for many of us to be reluctant to share our questions for fear that they seem too trivial. Alternatively, we may be reluctant to share our personal issues or problems because we do not want to look weak or inadequate. It is hard to reveal our vulnerabilities. One thing about self-study is that it clearly involves risk-taking and a level of vulnerability. Self-study requires a certain mindset or disposition to be willing to share and receive constructive criticism. Participants take risks sharing their work and personal views. You might recall in Chapter 2 and Chapter 3 that we discussed how self-study is open to public critique, collective, and interpersonal.

Self-study necessitates a disposition of openness to outside views, questions, and critique. The disposition of the collaborators should be one of open-mindedness to new ideas, different perspectives, and probing questions. Therefore, a climate of trust is essential to encourage a free flow of ideas. It takes practice being the supportive collaborator who provides

encouragement, while at the same time being a critical friend asking probing questions and critically analyzing the issues.

Situated inquiry

Our goal is for you to reflect and experience the many different ways to move beyond reflection to critical inquiry by practicing self-study in your teaching context. We believe that by doing so, you will develop not only habits of reflection but you will reframe your thinking about teaching as you consider the impact of the experience on your teaching. This reframing in turn leads to personal and professional growth and ways to improve your practice and schooling. As we discussed in Chapter 2, your questions, your role, and your reframing of practice are central to self-study. The dispositions of reflection, collaboration, openness, and situated inquiry are integral to methodology requirements.

Methodology Requirements

We draw upon the extensive work of LaBoskey (2004b), a leader in the field of self-study research, to provide a foundation for understanding the methodology of self-study. LaBoskey (2004b) outlines four requirements for practicing self-study:

> Self-study is self-initiated and focused on self. Its goal is self-improvement, and it "requires evidence of reframed thinking and transformed practice" (p. 859).

> Self-study is interactive and involves collaboration and interaction with colleagues, students, and the literature "to confirm or challenge our developing understandings" (p. 859).

> "Self-study employs multiple, primarily qualitative methods" . . . which "provide us with opportunities to gain different and thus more comprehensive perspectives on the educational processes under investigation" (p. 859).

> Self-study requires that we "formalize our work and make it available to our professional commu-

nity for deliberation, further testing, and judgment." "Self-study achieves validation through the construction, testing, sharing and re-testing of exemplars of teaching practice" (p. 860).

Methodology Components

In addition to the four requirements for self-study, LaBoskey (2004b) identifies three components of self-study methodology, first, pedagogical strategies, second, research design, and third, design representations. She reminds us that as teachers we have a pedagogical responsibility to continuously monitor our progress and justify the pedagogies we use. She points out that there must be a close connection between our pedagogy and our research methods.

Our research methods should be interactive and responsive to what and how we teach and must capture the complexity of what we do. Because our research methods vary and combine in order to capture this complexity, our representational modes may also vary. Therefore, along with the important connections between pedagogical strategies and research design, there should be a tight connection between our research design and our research representations. For this reason the representational modes for self-study are not restricted or confined to written reports, but may include other forms such as arts-based or performance-based representations. The critical point to keep in mind when distinguishing methodology from methods is that the methodology of self-study emphasizes the self as having central importance. Self-study defines the focus of the study, (i.e., the context and nature of a person's activity), not the way the study is carried out.

Methods of Self-Study

Methods (methodological approaches)

research procedures and techniques characteristic of a particular discipline or field of knowledge

We use the term **methods** in a broad way to refer to the procedures and techniques of the self-study discipline. As mentioned above, self-study methodology employs qualitative research methods, and the use of the method employed depends on the purpose of the study. Loughran (2004) notes, " . . .

the question/issue/concern under consideration invokes the use of a method(s) that is appropriate for uncovering evidence in accord with the purpose/intent of the study" (p. 17). As noted earlier in Chapter 1, we see self-study as having different purposes which drive the form the self-study takes.

In self-study we share numerous methods used in other forms of research. These methods may include: personal history, developmental portfolio self-study, memory work, arts-based self-study and collective self-study. Examples of these methods are included in the invitations to practice section of this chapter and in the References and Resources section. Within these methods, self-study teachers can also choose various techniques and/or medium to explore their questions, such as education-related life histories, narrative inquiry, autobiography, journaling, storytelling, video recordings of one's teaching, visual representations, performance, photography, or art installations (LaBoskey, 2004b, p. 814). The significant difference between self-study and other forms of qualitative research is that self-study may employ a variety of different methods while always maintaining a focus on the self.

Formal and Informal Approaches of Self-Study

In the following sections we discuss the different approaches to self-study, and explore the main features that differentiate informal self-study from formal self-study. Because the purpose of self-study influences one's approach, we invite the reader to consider why he/she is engaging in self-study.

Is your purpose for conducting self-study to contribute to the knowledge base of teaching by systematically studying and documenting your practice and then making your research public through presentation or publication in a formal context? If so, your self-study would be considered a **formal self-study approach,** which we will discuss more in-depth in the following chapter. On the other hand, are you more interested in focusing on self-improvement by solving your unique classroom dilemma rather than

Formal self-study approach

refers to a systematic research approach to explore one's practice which is made available to the professional community

publishing your findings? If your purpose for conducting self-study is to inquire into your teaching and your students' learning and not make your findings public, we refer to this as an **informal self-study approach.** Mills (2003) points out that teachers may have the desire to address and resolve their own particular problems, but for pragmatic reasons are not interested in publication. Similarly, preservice and inservice teachers may engage in self-study, but the intent or purpose of the exercise may not necessarily be to contribute to the knowledge base of teaching (Robinson, 1993).

Informal Self-Study Approach

We use the term informal self-study in a broad sense to include activities that provide practice in exploring one's teaching and learning using reflection as a critical dimension. This informal approach employs self-study methods (e.g., journaling, personal history papers, autobiographies), but does not necessarily involve formal data gathering, nor is it intended to be formally written up or made public. Informal self-study has many of the characteristics of formal self-study, but it is not subject to the criteria or the in-depth peer critique as required for formal reports such as master's or dissertation research (Ham & Kane, 2004). Informal self-study may be incorporated in preservice and inservice programs to encourage teachers to gain practice using strategies to reflect on and inquire into their beliefs and theories in practice.

We now move from the theory of self-study to discussing ways to apply it in your practice. We include invitations to practice to provide examples of ways for you to engage in self-study. If you decide that formal self-study serves your needs, then these informal activities can easily be extended to a formal self-study. That will depend on your purpose and your needs.

Invitations to Practice Informal Self-Study

We have designed these invitations to provide opportunities for you to practice sharing ideas, uncertainties, dilemmas of practice, and stretch your willingness to take risks. By doing so, you can gain "hands-on" experience engaging in self-study in an informal way. By personally engaging in these activities, you have the opportunity to discover the value of self-study for yourself. We hope that these invitations to practice will serve as opportunities to cultivate habits of self-study so that you internalize a self-study stance toward your teaching and your students' learning.

How can you develop this stance or disposition? We believe it can be done through practice in your specific context and with the support of colleagues. That is why we have included these invitations to practice. They are designed to provide opportunities to see the many different ways that you can develop and cultivate self-study skills. When you experience the value of collaborating, you will continue to interact with other teachers creating a culture of collaboration and professional inquiry.

Organization of the Invitations to Practice

Each one of the invitations includes elements of self-study and is organized in the following way: Purpose, Context, Wonderings/questions, Process, Data Collection, Collaboration, and Evidence of Impact. Here's an overview of what the elements include:

- The purpose explains the goals and objectives of the invitation.
- Please write in your context.
- The wonderings/questions are possible focus questions. We know you will have others to add to our list.
- The process section encompasses the procedures and the suggested steps of the activity.
- We encourage you to jot down the data that you decide to use for your data collection. One thing we have discovered in our work with teachers is that teachers collect considerable amounts of data about their students all the time. As researchers you have sources of data all around

you in the form of students' work, journals, your written observations of students, records of students' progress, individual conferences, class photographs, and/or videos. Additionally, you have lots of data about your teaching, such as lesson plans, rough notes about strategies you tried, meetings you attended, comments from other teachers, your yearly goal setting statements, and peer, mentor, and/or administrators' assessments. You may also have journals, stories, including life histories, autobiography, personal essays, or diaries.

- Collaboration entails suggestions, activities, and questions to encourage your collaboration with trusted colleagues. We have included a component called pair share which provides opportunities to practice the essential aspects of critical reflection and collaboration with openness.

- Finally, the evidence of impact is a place for you to reflect and write what evidence-based changes you note in your teaching and your students' learning after practicing an informal self-study. It includes your ongoing reflection and reframing or a feedback loop for your continued self-study. It is also a place you might revisit if you decide to conduct a formal data analysis through a formal self-study which we discuss later.

The examples included in the invitations to practice provide a variety of different self-study methods: first, the personal history self-study method second, the developmental portfolio self-study method; and third, the arts-based self-study method using visual representations. By including a number of different examples, you can see that self-study includes a broad array of approaches and is not limited to only a few specific techniques. The method you choose is driven by your interests, questions, and purpose. These invitations provide different ways to address your specific self-study purpose. You might recall that you may engage in self-study for, first, personal development, second, professional development, and/or, third, classroom and school improvement.

We would like to suggest you move to an invitation that you are interested in trying out and then return to others at a later time.

Self-Study for Personal Development

One self-study method that addresses the area of personal development is called the **personal history self-study method.** This method entails formative, contextualized experiences that have influenced teachers' thinking about teaching and their own practice. Historical and life experiences are used to prompt reflection for professional meaning-making and the reflections may take the form of narratives, journaling, correspondence, electronic mail exchanges, audiotaped discussions, videotapes of one's teaching, storytelling, memory work, emotion work, education-related life-histories, interviews, and multiple forms of artistic expression such as drawing, photography, poetry, and artistic installations. Although there are a wide variety of forms, the central focus of personal history self-study is on how one's personal experience can inform one's professional practice.

The personal history self-study invitation to practice illustrates how this can be done by critically reflecting on your personal experiences, which may include your personal histories and education-related life experiences. These experiences can have a direct impact on your beliefs about teaching and learning. Your personal self-study can involve exploring your identity as a teacher. Exploring your teacher identity might involve examining your teaching beliefs and exploring how your practices align with your beliefs. The following education-related life history invitation is an example of a personal history self-study method.

Personal history self-study method entails formative, contextualized experiences that have influenced teachers' thinking about teaching and their own practice

■ ■

Invitation to Practice
Personal History Self-Study Method

Everybody has a Story

(Adapted from the work of Bullough & Gitlin, 1995; Mitchell & Weber, 1999; Samaras, 2002).

Purpose

Although we can explore our teacher identity in numerous ways, this education-related life history is one way to explore how our personal learning experiences shape our professional practice. In Chapter 1, we mentioned that an education-related life history is a self-study activity that involves reflection on critical or nodal moments in one's learning past that may help to inform one's teaching.

Context

(You add your own personal context).

Wonderings/questions

- How have social and cultural influences shaped my development and that of my students?
- How can inquiry into my education-related life history inform my current practices?
- How can conducting personal history self-study assist me in understanding how my students' experiences have impacted and shaped their learning?

Process and Data Collection

1 Find a place to work alone.
2 Reflect back on a compelling education-related experience where you tried to learn something that was difficult for you. Visualize yourself as a novice learning a difficult skill such as learning to ride a bicycle, learning to swim, learning to drive. It can be a learning experience that occurred some time ago or occurred more recently. It might be an experience from a particular sit-

uation such as a mathematics class or from a situation outside of a school setting.

3　Write a narrative about that experience. The key is to write and describe your experience as a learner as specifically and fully as you can.

Below are some suggestions for reflecting on your learning experience:

- What was involved for you as you learned something new? As teachers, we have all also been learners. Think about what it means to you to be a learner.
- Try to focus on an example of an experience which stands out in its vividness, or as it was when it occurred.
- Revisualize the setting. Where are you? What's happening around you? Who else is involved? What's happening in the world? Does that matter to this story?
- Describe the experience as you live through it. Avoid causal explanations and generalizations. How old are you? What makes you remember this incident?
- Attend to how/what you felt physically as well as mentally. Describe the experience as fully as you can. Describe your feelings, mood, emotions, etc. Did you feel failure, fear, disappointment, or confusion?
- Avoid trying to glamorize your narrative. Use your own words and be honest with yourself.

Collaboration

4　Pair Share Session: Pair with a colleague and read your narrative.

5　Exchange places with your colleague and listen to his/her narrative.

6　Discuss what you hear in each other's narrative.

7　Identify and notice the data that emerge from your narrative. Is there evidence of particular themes in each narrative? Discuss the implications of your learning to your teaching.

Sustaining, Concluding, Extending Activities

8   Collective Self-Study
   - With a group of colleagues discuss and look at what you have identified. Have a discussion about the themes that stand out for you in each education-related life history.
   - Then select one of the themes and prepare a three-minute group creation and presentation of your choice, e.g., first, a skit, second, a series of monologues, third, an improvisation, or fourth, a tableau—a group's frozen still image that represents a significant theme. Present that to another group of colleagues.

Evidence of Impact

   - What role has culture played in your learning and teaching?
   - What did you discover about your difficult learning experience and its implications to your teaching?

Self-Study for Professional Development

Developmental portfolio self-study method

presents an opportunity to store, catalogue, and study one's professional growth over a certain time period

Another aspect of self-study involves inquiring into your professional growth and development as a teacher. A self-study method that we like to use for this purpose is the **developmental portfolio self-study method**. The developmental portfolio self-study method presents an opportunity to store, catalogue, and study your professional growth over a selected time period. The portfolio can contain your reflective journals, lessons, projects, papers, and your work with critical friends who help validate your findings (see Lyons & Freidus, 2004). It is a storehouse of data that you can use to document and analyze your teaching and your students' learning. The portfolio is a valuable self-study tool for studying your growth and development as a teacher.

■ ■

Invitation to Practice
Developmental Portfolio Self-Study Method

Partner Portfolios for Professional Development

Purpose

There are various ways we can explore our professional development. One way is the developmental portfolio self-study that enables us to uncover new and not always apparent dimensions of our teaching. Effective teaching involves continuous learning. Partner portfolios provide us with opportunities to inquire into our practice with critical friends/colleagues who help us reframe our thinking about teaching and learning. Critical friends provide support as well as a feedback loop to improve our practice and our students' learning.

Context

(You add your own personal context).

Wonderings/questions

- What would I like to be the focus or the foci of this growth document?
- What components of my teaching would I like to improve? What are my personal and professional goals?
- What span of time am I interested in studying? Why?

Process

1 Choose your developmental portfolio self-study focus. A developmental self-study portfolio typically spans a considerable period of time so you can examine the longitudinal nature of your professional development either broadly or with a specific focus. It can assist you in identifying the dilemmas encountered and changes over time. It may address a broad professional goal such as how to best and equitably inte-

grate technology in your classroom or a specific concern such as dealing with "difficult" students and/or parents.

2 Once you have selected your focus, decide on a timeline for data collection and what kinds of data you will collect, e.g., journals, videotaping of teaching, photographs of your classroom, notes from home visits, notes from phone call conversations, evaluations, and student feedback. Your portfolio can also include observations, lessons, projects, journals, audiotaped discussions with peers, mentor feedback, videotapes of your teaching, and/or student interviews. You might write about an experience, and/or an interaction that led you to a new way of seeing your teaching world. Multiple data sources serve to validate your findings.

3 Use a binder that allows you to insert and remove materials. Organize according to your focus. Add pockets for non-written sources such CDs, videos, student projects, etc.

Data Collection

4 Collect and date all data.

5 Read and re-read your data. Pay particular attention to any repeated statements, behaviors, and actions across your data set. Reflect on your work and learning. Read back through the items you have decided to collect in your developmental portfolio. Give yourself time and permission to reflect honestly and to study yourself as a learner and teacher. It is all right to change your philosophy and actions without incurring guilt over past practices and beliefs.

6 Analyze and write about your professional growth. Below are suggested questions to guide your data analysis:

- Look through your journals. Which entries stand out for you and why?
- What categories or common themes are evident in your looking back?
- Read back to your earlier viewpoints, beliefs,

and attitudes. Has anything changed? Remained the same? What factors and experiences do you believe contributed to the changes? What new insights have you gained about yourself?

- Is there evidence of reflective thinking about your new understandings regarding teaching and students' learning?
- What were your dilemmas?
- What metaphor best captures who you are as a teacher?
- Are there paradoxes that capture the essence of your work? These might include: disharmony/harmony; despair/hope; status quo/ change; struggle/success; or consistency/ possibilities.
- What was your greatest ah-ha or discovery?
- How do you see yourself as a teacher at this stage of your professional development?
- Do you think your colleagues would describe you differently from when they first started working with you? What might they say?
- How would you assess your participation with students, parents, colleagues?
- What do you want to continue doing?
- What are you still struggling with to understand about yourself and/or others?
- What are your professional wishes and hopes yet unfulfilled?

Collaboration

7   Next, using your notations from your data analysis, write a letter to a trusted colleague about your professional journey to date.

8   Pair Share Session
- Engage in several planned conversations with your colleague about your professional development.
- Use active listening, i.e., listening for each other without judgment and without personal agendas.
- Share personal stories you might have included

in your portfolio.
- Take turns listening and hearing each other's perspectives.

Sustaining, Concluding, Extending Activities

9   Extend the pair share session to a group of colleagues. Form a **Talk Trust Group** and continue to meet and discuss the changes you document over time.

10 You might also use an online learning environment or a chat room for extending your conversations and invite others into that conversation to gain their perspectives.

Talk Trust Group
a group of trusted colleagues who meet regularly to share their developmental self-study portfolios

Evidence of impact

- Talk about your professional development as a result of this developmental portfolio self-study method.
- What changes have you noted in your teaching over time? How did you frame and reframe your practice?
- Did you seek validation with your colleague on agreed upon categories and themes?
- Revisit each other's portfolio together at a later time and celebrate the changes you discover.

Self-Study for Classroom and School Improvement

Ultimately, our work as self-study teachers is to improve learning for students. This may involve inquiring into our reasons of why we do what we do. How does what I do impact my students' learning? These inquiries into our teaching can be conducted in a number of different ways. They can include narrative inquiry approaches such as education-related life-histories, autobiography, metaphors, personal essays, and/or poetry. They can also include visual representations in arts-based self-study such as the one we share with you next.

■ ■

Invitation to Practice
Arts-Based Self-Study Method—Visual Representations

Mapping My Classroom

Purpose

Arts-based self-study method
promotes and provokes self-reflection, critical analysis, and dialogue about one's understanding of teaching through the arts; includes a wide range of art forms such as visual representation, portraits, improvisation, performance, and photography

Dialectical unity
our capacity to relate ourselves and other as other than, in advance of, our professional development

Concept maps
representations of one's theories and practices

Arts-based self-study method promotes and provokes self-reflection, critical analysis, and dialogue about improving one's teaching through the arts. The arts are a conduit for **dialectical unity** or our capacity to relate to ourselves and others (see Holzman, 1997). Arts-based self-study teachers use a wide range of art forms to represent and reinterpret, construct and deconstruct meaning, and communicate their study of teaching as they make it public. It can take many forms including visual/image based arts, (e.g., portraits, performance, photography, video documentary, art installations, multi-media representations, films, drawings, cartoons, graffiti, signs, cyber graphics, diagrams, and concept maps (see Weber & Mitchell, 2002).

Concept maps are visual representations of what you know and what you want to know more about (see Novak & Gowin, 1984). They are ways of representing and thinking about your theories and practice (Samaras, 2002). Concepts are ideas derived from your conscious perception and classification of facts and events based on their common characteristics. Concept maps are artistic and cognitive tools that allow you to discover and demonstrate conceptual connections between and within concepts in a self-study. How you design your concept map is up to you. You can create your map using circles, boxes, pictures, or symbols of big ideas; use text alone; text within boxes; hand-drawn or computer drawn; black and white or color-coded, etc. There are no predetermined categories or concepts. The self-study teacher draws his/her understandings based on the connections noted in the concept map.

Context

(You add your own personal context)

Wonderings/questions

- What can I learn about my teaching by mapping my classroom environment?
- What type of learning culture do I want to co-create with my students?
- If someone else "read" my classroom and observed my teaching, what might they conclude about my teaching beliefs?

Process and data collection

1 Be a participant and an observer of your own classroom. Reflect on what you see. Seeing is more than observing. Be open and suspend your assumptions. Look at your students from different vantage points, on different days of the week, and at different times of day. Notice students interacting with peers, when they are alone, and during various classroom activities.

2 Draw a pre-action concept map of your classroom's groups, sub-groups, and the placement of you within that grouping before attempting any changes in your classroom. Here are some ideas to get you started:

  - Map the social theater of your classroom including seating arrangements, room layout, where things are located, and resources available.
  - What are the relationships and interactions between you and your students?
  - What are the power relationships between you and your students, and among students themselves?
  - Are there differentiated rules for individual students?
  - Are there subcultures or groups in your classroom?
  - What are the positions of participants? Are there leaders and followers? Do those positions change? When? Why?

- Consider the interactions and social events between students.
- What are the rights and responsibilities of students and the teacher?
- Describe the interactions between yourself and students including the norms and sanctions.
- Are students responsible for their own behavior?
- Is there a shared culture of monitoring behavior?
- Who decides when activities are begun and how long they last?
- Map what the classroom looks like when you are teaching and when you are not teaching.
- What does this mapping and reflection tell you about your classroom?

3 Remapping: Decide what you want to know and/or change and begin to implement those changes. Develop strategies for that change.

4 Keep a record of your strategies and actions for change and keep notes on the consequences of your actions over time.

5 Collect data on this process as you come to better understand the dynamics of your classroom.

6 Next, draw a post-action concept map after implementing your strategies. Pre-action and post-action concept maps are useful for formative and summative assessment to see the differences before and after you take action. You may also find metaphors useful to capture significant changes and enter those words into and around your post-action concept map frame.

7 Place your pre-action and post-action concept maps side by side. Analyze them for differences. Prepare to share any shifts and differences you can identify with a colleague.

Collaboration

8 Pair Share Session
- Take time to examine each other's concept maps. On a visual plane, what is most obvi-

ous to you?

- Have a discussion about what you each notice.
- Actively listen to your colleague.

Sustaining, concluding, extending activities

9. Group Work

Continue the conversation with a grade-level or discipline team.

Evidence of impact

- What awareness has this activity raised for you about your knowledge of your teaching and classroom?
- What observations triggered your interest in changing your classroom?
- What difference did your remapping make for your students' learning?

Now that you have had a chance to try out some different examples of informal self-study, we hope these invitations to practice self-study will encourage you to engage in further self-study. We have included additional invitations to practice in the References and Resource section. There you will find invitations for memory work, **collective self-study method**, and other arts-based self-study methods including portraits, improvisation, performance, and photography. In the final chapter we will discuss formal self-study and provide examples of how to conduct and write a formal self-study. However, before we do that, we leave you with a thought regarding the possibility and ease of making your informal study a formal one.

Collective self-study method

involves a group of people who collaboratively design, implement, and evaluate a self-study project

Informal to Formal Self-Study

Informal self-study activities like the ones above can be a great starting point for taking your self-study to a formal level. Your study can be expanded to include systematic data collection and analysis of the evidence of the impact. Let's take a look at the self-study work of Claudia Mitchell (2006) as a good example of that. Many teachers keep personal journals and diaries, and numerous informal self-study activities may include journal work. What do you think would happen if you systematically analyzed your journals?

Claudia writes, "There is a large old wooden trunk in my study that contains a cardboard box full of my journals—the data, the raw material. These date back to 30 June 1968 and go into the 1990s . . ." (p. 119). Nearly 40 years after she first started her journal, Claudia decided to conduct a formal self-study by incorporating memory work techniques to explore her teacher development over her lengthy career. She examined the ways that her self-study research contributes to her current work with teachers.

The first step of her formal self-study was to decide what data to use and how to reduce it to a manageable inquiry. After much reflection in the process of assembling her raw data, she decided to concentrate on a seven-year period of teaching as a junior high English teacher in a small fishing village in Nova Scotia. She states, "I focus on this period chiefly because it is the time when I most called myself 'teacher'" (p. 120).

Claudia's next step in the research process was to translate her personal documents into what she calls "artefacts" for study. She organized the journals by date and filed them for ease in accessing them. Then she weighed the possibilities of using various analytic procedures. She questioned what kind of self-study she wanted to engage in, and explored what benefits lay in taking different directions. Dealing with the large amount of data she states, "I find myself wanting to work with just one or two entries, but at the same time being intrigued by the vastness. . . ." (p. 121). She contemplated if she should count how many words or how many pages she had written; or perhaps she should make note of how many different topics she wrote about; identify what recurring topics are embedded in the journals. Perhaps she should make note of the most interesting topics to re-read or the topics that lent themselves to analysis.

As she read and re-read her journals, she began to make sense of what the teaching world looked like to her then. She began taking notes and looking for patterns or themes. She shares a journal which expressed her disappointment with her teaching.

> At present I am very depressed about the school and my role there. In truth, it is all very disturbing—my material is so interesting—particularly English, but it is coming across poorly, dully, mediocrely. Tomorrow I should talk to the hellions but I wonder if I will even get their attention long enough to say anything. (p. 123)

As she reread her journal entries, she noticed how she wove together the personal details of her life, such as buying a farm, getting a loan, having children, and starting her graduate studies. Her analysis revealed that her later journals were briefer. They also showed how much she enjoyed teaching.

In the interpretive phase of her research she notes that reading about herself as a teacher from 21 to 28 years old reminded her that many of her education students are in that same age range. This realization gave her insight into the interpretive lens through which many of her students make sense of their teaching. She noticed the counter-culture nature of her teaching, her "take on the world" attitude, and the context of her Mother Earth living style. Now she asks her education students to keep journals of their teaching and to look at the changes over time. In her work in South Africa investigating how gender, HIV, and AIDS are being addressed in classrooms, she encourages her practicing teachers to see their field notes as journals and data. In essence, Claudia gained a deeper connection between her work as schoolteacher and her current work as a teacher educator. She sees how she continues to embrace a "take on the world" attitude as she works to raise people's consciousness about teaching, women's issues, and social reform.

In the next chapter we will discuss formal self-study and provide examples of how to conduct and

write a formal self-study. You will have the opportunity to consider designing a formal self-study that may build upon an informal self-study project.

Arts-based self-study method—promotes and provokes self-reflection, critical analysis, and dialogue about one's understanding of teaching through the arts; includes a wide range of art forms such as visual representations, portraits, improvisation, performance, and photography

Collective self-study method—involves a group of people who collaboratively design, implement, and evaluate a self-study project

Concept maps—representations of one's theories and practices

Developmental portfolio self-study method—presents an opportunity to store, catalogue, and study one's professional growth over a selected time period

Dialectical unity—our capacity to relate to ourselves and others as other than, and in advance of, our professional development (see Holzman, 1997)

Formal self-study approach—refers to a systematic research approach to exploring one's practice which is made available to the professional community

Informal self-study approach—includes activities that provide practice in exploring one's teaching and learning using reflection as a critical dimension; does not necessarily involve formal data gathering

Memory work—a self-study method used to represent autobiographical inquiry with critical and reflective revisiting

Methodology—a body of practices, procedures, and guidelines used by those who work in a discipline or engage in an inquiry

Methods (methodological approaches)—research procedures and techniques characteristic of a particular discipline or field of knowledge

Personal history self-study method—entails formative, contextualized experiences that have influenced teachers' thinking about teaching and their own practice

Talk Trust Group—a group of trusted colleagues who meet regularly to share their developmental self-study portfolios

Formal Self-Study of Teaching

Quickwrite

Identify a major research question. What do you wonder and care deeply about in your teaching? How does this research question relate to your lived experience and personal history? How might your research efforts contribute to the knowledge base of teaching and learning?

As we mentioned in Chapter 4, we use the phrase *formal self-study* to refer to a systematic approach to exploring one's practice. Formal self-studies include critical inquiry that emphasizes a formalization of one's work by applying research methods to the study of one's teaching and making the study available to the professional community. This objective generally involves a systematic, written study of one's practice. This formal approach may include master's theses, dissertations, conference papers and presentations, and peer-reviewed journal articles. The purpose or intent of formal self-study is to be made public and presented to a broad audience. Formal self-

study makes the research accessible to other members of the scholarly community and provides opportunities for knowledge generation and expanding the scholarship of teaching. Formal self-studies, conducted by teachers, graduate students, and academics, make a valuable contribution to one's personal and professional learning. Self-study generates knowledge about teacher learning and contributes to the knowledge base of teaching and learning. As we disseminate self-study research, new discoveries and findings trigger additional research, thus making a contribution to the broader teaching community.

In a formal self-study we draw upon qualitative research methods as the organizing structure. Scholars within the field of self-study have identified criteria or guidelines for reporting self-study (Barnes, 1998; Bullough & Pinnegar, 2001; Feldman, 2003; Loughran & Northfield, 1998; LaBoskey, 2004b). Ham & Kane (2004) point out that in the self-study literature "the discussion of the key characteristics of research often revolve around the various conventionalized, some would way ritualized, processes of data gathering, analysis/synthesis and presentation that accompany a claim to public knowledge" (p. 113). They go on to say that self-study written papers and conventional research reports often use "headings like 'Theoretical framework,' 'Objectives of the study,' 'Methods,' 'Data sources,' 'Findings,' and 'Implications of the study' (Ham & Kane, 2004, p. 113).

Guidelines for Conducting a Formal Self-Study

We do not want this section to be seen as too prescriptive, but rather instructive to you as a preservice teacher, inservice teacher, or graduate student who may be interested in writing a formal self-study paper. We acknowledge that conducting formal self-study does not preclude non-traditional forms of presentation. However, in the case of graduate students and academics, the mode of representation is often written, formal papers, and therefore we focus here on conventional written research reports.

Research Assumptions

We start by addressing certain assumptions about research and attempt to dispel some of these assumptions that also apply to self-study. In our teaching we have found that students often maintain beliefs about what constitutes "real" research. When they hear the word "research" they think of research from a quantitative standpoint and envision scientific experiments, statistics, and experimental guidelines. From their discussions and questions about research, one notion that emerges is a strongly held belief that research must begin with a hypothesis. Their initial research questions often reveal their belief that the study must prove something. For example, many students pose questions that compare one approach to another such as: "Is this method of teaching reading better than that method of teaching reading?"

Research as Discovery

To dispel these assumptions or beliefs, we want to emphasize the view of self-study research as a process of ongoing discovery. Viewing research as a process of discovery leads the researcher to focus on the complex interactions that occur during the learning and teaching process. Think of your research as a journey toward greater understanding of one's self, one's teaching, as well as one's students.

Formal self-study requires rigor and is empirically grounded. Although the purpose of self-study research may be somewhat different from other types of research, the data gathering and analysis procedures for self-study are similar to qualitative research methods (Ham & Kane, 2004). To conduct valid self-study research, you need to know how to systematically collect multiple sources of data and how to analyze your data using appropriate methods. Finally, you need to know how to align your analysis and interpretation with your research questions and theoretical framework (Cochran-Smith & Zeichner, 2005).

The Process of Formal Self-Study Research

Formal self-study involves a systematic process that starts with discovering and posing the questions, gathering the data, and analyzing the data to find answers to the questions. When you begin your self-study research, the initial step is to find your questions. The *Invitations to Practice* in the previous chapter may give you some ideas about what you might like to study. Frequently, one of the hardest things and one of the biggest hurdles in conducting your research is to identify your research questions. Here are some tips for finding your research question/s.

Wondering

Start by asking yourself, "What do I wonder about, what is something that intrigues me?" These wonderings may come from your daily teaching. Your questions may come from a puzzling or nagging incident, something someone said, observations that surprise you, tensions in your class, or from individual students that puzzle you (Hubbard & Power, 1999). They may be about yourself, your teaching and/or your students. You can start with an open-ended inquiry as you question your assumptions about what is actually happening in your classroom. "What's going on here? What happens when I systematically study my teaching?" One way to help identify your questions is by keeping a journal for several weeks. After you have written your reflections, read through your journal entries to see what topics or questions have emerged.

Refining the questions

Be willing to question and explore issues or dilemmas that have no set answers or whose answers you are not sure about. We encourage you to start with open-ended questions that may allow for other possible questions and new insights to emerge. We encourage you to pose questions that are open-ended enough so that you can see the complexity of the learning and teaching process as it unfolds. We suggest that you avoid questions that compare one approach to another, or questions that are too tightly framed. Don't start out trying to prove something or ask research questions that confirm teaching practices you already think are good or bad practices (Hubbard & Power, 1999). Be aware that during the process, the nature of the questions may change and shift in focus. As you search for answers to your questions, the result may involve seeing yourself and your students in different ways. Along the way, you want to ask yourself, "Why do I want to study this?" When you ask this question, you are addressing your research purpose.

Example of refining your questions

Let's look at Alexis, a preservice teacher, and the process she went through as she refined her research question. The purpose of Alexis' study was to systematically explore her questioning strategies in her mathematics classroom and to see how her questions impacted her students' critical thinking. Notice how Alexis' questions shift focus along the way. Her initial questions focus on studying herself and her questioning strategies. She begins with:

- What kinds of questions do I ask?
- How does my questioning impact my students' critical thinking?
- How can I get my students to be critical thinkers?
- What is the impact of my questions on my students' understanding of math?

At the outset of the study, the focus of the research was on "teacher talk." Audiotapes of the Alexis' questioning strategies were recorded and transcribed. However, as the study progressed, she realized how important it was to also focus on "student talk." This is an example of how the questions and focus of the study may shift. It also illustrates the interactive nature of self-study and the complex interaction of the teacher and the learners. New questions emerged when Alexis realized she could not effectively study her questioning without including "student

talk." Her later questions demonstrate how she refined and expanded her research questions:

- What happens when I pay attention to the students' questions?
- What happens when I pay attention to the students' answers?
- How do the students demonstrate critical thinking?
- What's going on in the students' heads?
- How can I tell if the students are developing critical thinking skills?
- What happens when I change my questioning strategies?
- How do my students' responses change when I ask probing questions?

Notice the open-ended nature of the questions. Many of the questions start with phrases like "What happens when. . . ." or "How does . . . ." These types of questions allow for the researcher to be open-minded to the possibilities that may emerge during the inquiry.

Review of the literature

We mentioned that a critical aspect of your study is identifying your questions. While you are identifying and refining your questions, read what other researchers have done. Reviewing the research literature (academic journals, books, handbooks of research, and so on) can help you locate studies related to your research question or topic. Search for studies that are connected to your purpose and framework. If you are not sure what your framework is, the literature can provide support and give you ideas for a theoretical framework that fits your study. As you search the literature, do not forget to turn to the bibliography or references in the paper/article, because they can be a valuable resource for finding additional studies relevant to your research. The literature can provide you with researchers' definitions of key terms as well as examples of data sources, data collection methods, and procedures for implementing your research. You may locate a study that has a research design that could be modified to fit the goals of your study. The literature can also provide useful examples of how to organize your data and write your paper. Research studies are valuable resources for triggering new ideas that may not have occurred to you.

Methods

Data collection

As you refine your questions, you will begin to identify your research methods. Ask yourself: what data will I collect? What are possible sources of data? This is where your methods section begins to take shape. You can begin writing parts of this section by describing your participants, how they were selected, and your procedures for collecting data. Some examples of data sources may include your journal, student journals, free writes, videotapes, conference notes, evaluation data, photos, observations/field notes, anecdotal notes, and interviews. One thing to keep in mind is to collect more than one source of data. When you collect data from a variety of data sources, you are triangulating your data. Triangulating your data across sources is a way of strengthening the validity of your study. Some possible examples of triangulation of data would include comparing your journal entries with transcribed audio or videotapes of your teaching, as well as student data. Later in this chapter we provide an example of a formal self-study that involves multiple sources of data.

Data analysis

The next step after you have determined what data you will collect is to decide how you will analyze your data. Which data will require quantitative analysis? Which data sources will require qualitative analysis? Generally self-study involves qualitative data, but you may also have quantitative data. You can start your analysis by engaging and immersing yourself in systematic and thoughtful analysis.

Read and reread the data you have collected, e.g., your journal entries, observation notes, and student writing.

Compile and code surveys, interviews, and journal notes. Listen to your audiotapes and transcribe them. View your videotapes and take detailed notes. Start the process of coding your data by writing questions in the margins, assigning color codes, notes to self, and highlighting patterns and themes that emerge. Read and reread what you have saved and coded. Identify quotes or statements that support those themes. We have included tables later in the chapter that provide examples of themes that were derived from the analyses of journals and videotapes. As you read over your data and identify themes or patterns, ask yourself if you see changes in your thinking, your students' thinking, your students' behavior. Have your assumptions about teaching or your students shifted?

One thing to keep in mind is that the research process is not as neatly linear as it appears in the research outlines. Expect the unexpected and be open to new ideas, student misconceptions, and new understandings. Keep in mind that changes may occur, and more questions may emerge or shift as you are engaged in your research.

Writing up the Formal Research

Articulating your research takes time and focus, but here are some suggestions to guide you. Begin by outlining the chapters and subsections. Consider what will fit in each particular section. For example, in your introduction, start writing by talking about what inspired your study: what you wondered about and describe how the study took shape. State the purposes of your study. Describe your context and the participants.

In the methods section, discuss the data you collected and how you collected them. In the data analysis section, read and reread what you have written and coded. Look for themes or patterns in the data. Then look for evidence to support the themes or patterns you have identified. Start to write a draft of your findings. Put it in your own words. Do not get bogged down by trying to use scholarly language and educational jargon. Just start writing and let the ideas flow.

Lessons learned

As you synthesize your data, ask yourself what this information is telling you about your teaching, about your students' learning, about your classroom, or the specific issue you are studying. What is new here? What are the critical events or activities that provide evidence of change? How will this new insight impact my teaching, my thinking, my assumptions, my practice? Is there evidence of reframing or transformation in your thinking? Discuss what you learned from conducting your self-study.

Example of a formal self-study

The above sections provided a step-by-step discussion and guidelines for the process involved in conducting your study. In the next section we present excerpts from a preservice teacher's master's thesis as an example of a formal self-study. Using a series of tables, we provide an outline to guide you through the research process. Table 1 helps you see the steps that the researcher went through as he developed and conducted the study. Tables 2, 3, and 4 illustrate the data sources and depict how the various data sources were analyzed. We include these tables to help you visualize the process as we lead you through the research steps for conducting a formal self-study. For those of you who would like to know more about the self-study, a modified version of the paper is presented after Tables 1 to 4.

Table 1 outlines the research process from beginning to end. The table briefly discusses the data analysis and findings. The rest of the tables provide a more in-depth analysis of the main data sources: the dialogue journal and videotaped analyses.

TABLE 1: OUTLINE OF THE SELF-STUDY RESEARCH PROCESS

Research Guidelines	Description of the process
Finding the questions	**What do I wonder about?** The initial research questions arose from the preservice teacher's frustrations about his teaching and his students' behavior. • What is going wrong with my teaching? • Why don't the students follow directions? • Why aren't the students motivated? • Why don't they do their homework?
Refining the questions	**How can I focus my questions?** The preservice teacher posed open-ended research questions. • What happens when I examine my teaching? • What happens when I change my approach to the students? • How does what I do impact the students' behavior? By asking open-ended questions, new issues and questions may emerge.
Identifying methods Who? What? When? How?	**What data will I collect?** Ask yourself: • Who are the participants in the study? • What data will I collect? • When and how will I collect my data? This is where you begin to lay out your methods section. In this study the following research methods were identified. • Who are the participants? *Preservice teacher and students.* • What is being studied? *Preservice teacher systematically studies his teaching and students' learning.* • When does study take place? *Over a period of two semesters of student teaching.* • How will I collect my data? *Videotape my teaching; reflect on my teaching; document student behavior. The actual data sources included the student teacher/mentor teacher dialogue journal, teaching videotapes, assignments, and observation/field notes.* Note: Multiple sources of data were used to triangulate the data to increase the validity of the findings. The data sources objectively document the preservice teacher's development and provide evidence of his willingness "to scratch beneath the surface" and analyze what he was doing and what its effect was on his students.
Analyzing the data	How will I analyze the data? • *Compile and code the dialogue journal.* • *Transcribe and code videotapes. Compare and contrast videotapes from semester 3 and 4. (See Tables 3 and 4).* • *Compile and code observation notes/reflections.* **Dialogue journal analysis** The preservice teacher read and reread the coded data looking for trends, patterns, themes, or categories. Using the constant

Research Guidelines	Description of the process
	comparison method, he identified seven themes/areas of concern that emerged from his analysis of his dialogue journal. The themes included engagement, structure, consistency/follow through, setting routines, assessment, instructional strategies, and relationship to students' prior knowledge. He analyzed these themes and their relationship to student engagement and learning (see Table 2). **Videotape analysis** The preservice teacher systematically analyzed two videotapes (third semester/fourth semester) of his teaching using four of the themes that emerged from his analysis of the dialogue journal: engagement, structure, consistency/follow through, and setting routines. Using the four themes, he categorized student and teacher behaviors observed on the videotape and analyzed how his lack of student engagement, structure, consistency/follow through, and routines impacted student behavior and learning. He compared and contrasted the instructional changes he implemented in his fourth semester and the impact on increased student engagement, time on task, and a focus on learning.
Conclusions/ Lessons learned	Findings included the following: • Shift in thinking from his earlier position that the students control what is happening in the classroom to his awareness of how the behavior of the teacher impacts the students' behavior. • Specific instructional behaviors resulted in increased student engagement, time on task and a focus on learning. • Attitude shift from a sense of helplessness to one of taking responsibility for his teaching. • Moved to a disposition of open-mindedness and began to see other viewpoints. • Shifted from a sense of helplessness to one of taking responsibility for his teaching. • Framed and reframed his thinking about teaching. He began to take responsibility for his actions and was more wholehearted about his commitment to teaching. He moved from the stance of student to teacher.

Dialogue Journal

The preservice teacher and the cooperating teacher maintained a dialogue journal throughout the third semester of student teaching. The cooperating teacher observed the preservice teacher's lessons and wrote comments/observations about the lessons. The pre-service teacher analyzed the dialogue journal by read-

TABLE 2: DIALOGUE JOURNAL ANALYSIS

Category	Description	Findings
Engagement	Keeping students active throughout the class period Grabbing students' attention with various activities that are broken into ten to fifteen minute blocks Identifying which activities are engaging and how to improve student engagement in the classroom	Continuously engaging students shows that the students' learning is valued for the whole period
Structure	Providing my academic and behavioral expectations for each assignment Responding and stating the objectives for each lesson Answering why are we doing this	Clearly providing my expectations helps reduce student confusion and frustration Reducing student confusion and frustration permits more opportunities for student learning Stating my objectives assures the importance and validity of my lesson and assignments to the students and to myself
Consistency/ Following Through	Giving consequences when academic and behavioral expectations are not met Being stern when giving consequences Keeping an eye out for problematic academic and behavioral habits Be consistent in giving and the type of consequences when problematic academic and behavioral habits are exemplified	Students will continuously test the types of behaviors the teacher will permit If the teacher does not follow through and is not consistent with his or her consequences, then he or she is not clearly communicating to his or her students of what are his or her behavioral expectations
Setting Routines	Setting routines should be done before, during, and after the lessons	Improves the efficiency of the class by structuring the things students should perform throughout the class.
Assessment	Watching whether students comprehend the ideas presented in my lessons Utilizing check questions and student faces to assess whether student learning is occurring	Even though I may think I am doing a thorough job in explicating my ideas, the students may not think so Continuously assess students' learning in order to reduce confusion and frustrations
Relationship to Students' Prior Knowledge	Improving the students' understanding of my lesson's topics by relating how these topics are a part of or affect the students' lives	Being able to relate to the students' lives provides a foundation to scaffold or enhance more information

ing through the comments over and over to discover recurring areas of concern and to generalize the areas into themes. Seven recurring themes emerged from his analyses. These areas included:

1 engagement;
2 structure;
3 consistency/follow through;
4 setting routines;
5 assessment;

6   instructional strategies;

7   relationship to students' prior knowledge.

The first column of the table lists the themes. The second column identifies general descriptions of the themes and examples of the cooperating teacher's comments taken from the dialogue journal. The third column includes the analyses of these themes and the preservice teacher's new insights and findings.

Videotape Analysis—Semester Three

Other valuable sources of data besides the dialogue journal were videotapes of the preservice

TABLE 3: THIRD-SEMESTER VIDEO ANALYSIS

Category	Description	Findings
Engagement	Several students are disengaged Two girls interrupt my lecture by walking around the classroom. One girl looks at her water bottle for most of the period A girl and a boy at least twice fight over school supplies	Lack of structure and consequences conveys to the students that learning is not important in my classroom
Structure	No agenda was explicated No purpose for the lecture as discussed	Students had no clue of what was expected of them because I did not give the appropriate structure to the lesson
Consistency/ Following Through	I stopped teaching at least seven times totaling about three minutes I discussed the students' behaviors in a mundane lecture for roughly four minutes	Total learning time wasted in this lesson because of misbehaviors is seven minutes Part of the problem is that I provided no consequence for wasting class time, except for wasting more class time with a lecture on the students' behaviors
Setting Routines	Students did not follow the learning log at the beginning of class Students required several seconds before they responded to me looking at my watch	Consistent consequences are not given when students do not meet my expectations

teacher recorded during his third and fourth semesters of teaching. As part of his self-study, the preservice teacher analyzed videotapes of his teaching from both semesters to explore areas of growth. Table 3 shows how the analysis was conducted. The preservice teacher framed the analysis using four of the themes that emerged from his previous dialogue journal analysis. The themes of, first, engagement; second, structure; third, consistency/following through; and, fourth, setting routines were used to systematically analyze the videotape of his teaching.

The first column lists the four themes. The second column contains a description of observations of student and teacher behaviors on the videotape. The third column includes the analyses of these themes and his new insights and findings. The descriptions of the observations of the students' behavior and the preservice teacher's actions in the second and third columns reveal the honest and critical analysis of the video by the preservice teacher. His findings illustrate how he made himself vulnerable as he reflected on and analyzed his teaching.

Videotape Analysis—Semester Four

Table 4 shows the fourth semester videotape analysis. Once again the themes of engagement, structure, consistency/follow through and setting routines were used to systematically analyze the videotapes of his teaching. The first column lists the four themes. The second column contains a description of observations of student and teacher behaviors on the videotape. The third column includes the analyses of these themes and his new insights and findings. The analyses of his third and fourth semester videotapes provide a comparison and contrast of the behavioral changes he implemented in his teaching. The fourth semester video analysis illustrates the changes that the student teacher implemented in his teaching. The findings suggest how he framed and reframed his teaching as a result of his systematic study of his teaching.

TABLE 4: FOURTH-SEMESTER VIDEO ANALYSIS

Category	Description	Findings
Engagement	Students were assigned tasks throughout the lesson. For instance, the boys must monitor their behaviors and a girl from each row must answer one of my questions Student-centered activities, such as Bernoulli's Lab Stations, were provided	By assigning every student a task, most students remained focused Student-oriented activities, such as labs, made the students active participants of their learning
Structure	The agenda was written and verbally given at the beginning of the class Detailed instructions were stated for the Bernoulli's Lab Stations	The agenda and explicit instructions provided the students with the objectives that were to be accomplished and how these objectives were going to be achieved
Consistency/ Following Through	The students' misbehaviors had to be addressed only three times	Reinforcing consequences of misbehaviors reduced the amount of time wasted on checking the students' behaviors

Example of a Formal Self-Study Paper

What follows is a modified version of the preservice teacher's self-study. We include it here to provide you with a more complete picture of the process of self-study and what a formal paper might include.

Rowan's Formal Self-Study

This is my story of becoming a science teacher. It is a story that resulted from a challenging, and at times, frustrating journey as a preservice teacher. During my two years in the master's in teaching program, I struggled to find my identity as a teacher. I encountered many up and downs, and questioned my ability to be a successful teacher. During my student teaching semester, the image of the teacher I thought I would become was shaken. No matter how hard I tried, it seemed as if my efforts were not enough. Students didn't listen to me, they didn't do their homework, and I began to dread going to school. I wondered what was going wrong with my

teaching. Was it the students? Or was it me? In order to find solutions to my problems, I decided to systematically study my preservice teaching experiences. This story is an account of the obstacles and challenges that I encountered on my journey. It is a story of my personal and professional growth as a preservice teacher. I begin the story by providing background and the context for the study.

Background

As a secondary science preservice teacher in a master's in teaching program, I was involved in university-based professional studies seminars, field-based experiences, and site-based seminars. The program emphasized inquiry, reflection, and collaboration, and involved extensive field experiences in the context of a professional development high school setting. As a preservice teacher I spent three semesters at the professional development school. During the first semester, I observed and participated in a variety of classrooms, and interacted with the teachers and students. In the second semester I continued to participate in the school for fifteen hours per week and taught two three-week units. During the third semester I taught three classes for the entire semester under the guidance of a mentor teacher. In the fourth semester I taught full-time as an intern teacher with support and guidance from an intern mentor and a university supervisor.

Context of the study

My first semester was marked by a keen interest in learning. I had a pretty clear idea of the type of teacher I wanted to be. I believed in "hands-on" participatory learning. I was interested in motivating my students by creating activities and assignments which involved the learners and would promote the joy of learning. I did not believe in lecturing to the students.

During the second semester I was still enthusiastic about teaching. I worked with two cooperating teachers and planned and taught two three-week units. In my first unit teaching experience, I had a comfortable relationship with my cooperating teacher and enjoyed the experience. However, in my second unit teaching experience, things did not go so well and I became frustrated. I became more and more concerned about how the students viewed me. My confidence was negatively affected and I began to question my desire to be a teacher. I realized that I had high expectations for myself as a teacher. I stepped into the teaching program with delusions of grandeur. I pictured myself wooing my students with fantastic demonstrations, and teaching with universal enthusiasm. I saw myself enticing my students to learn as much as my teachers did for me. When my performance did not match my expectations, I was frustrated. Here is what I wrote in my evaluation at the end of the second semester:

> For my unit I had students that were not motivated by my teaching. They continuously grumbled and argued about the amount of work that I assigned them. Their frustrations turned into mumbling on how much I was a bad teacher. This severely shell-shocked the image of the masterful teacher I saw myself. At the end of the unit, I doubted whether I wanted to become a teacher. These doubts continued even as I began my third semester in the program.

During the third semester, I taught three physics classes in the classroom of my cooperating teacher. During the summer prior to the third semester, I collaboratively planned my first physics unit with my cooperating teacher. When I started teaching, I remember feeling overwhelmed by the planning and paperwork from the outset. As time went on I began to feel overwhelmed with grading, writing lesson plans, and managing student behavior. I continued to write detailed lesson plans, even though my cooperating teacher encouraged me to lighten up and streamline my lesson plans.

Eventually I became more anxious and stressed. I resorted to lecturing the students. I ignored the students' off-task behavior as long as possible. At

that point I began to feel flustered and I would raise my voice and resort to punitive behaviors. The students resented this and began to tune me out. I felt as if it didn't matter what I did because the students didn't want to cooperate. I felt like it was the students who had control over what happened in the class, not me.

My university supervisor kept encouraging me to reflect on my experiences and either discuss them with my cooperating teacher or write about them in my dialogue journal. I resisted because reflection was uncomfortable for me. I do not enjoy revealing my feelings because it goes against the image of a logical, unbiased scientist. Therefore, questioning my feelings seemed unimportant and unintelligent. I can recall my university supervisor asking how I felt during and after a lesson and not being able to answer her because I did not feel comfortable sharing my feelings.

I was not willing to explore alternative explanations for the students' behavior. My perceptions of myself and teaching gradually became more and more negative. I pointed blame at many external factors: the students, the counselors, parents, my cooperating teacher, and my university supervisor for my difficulties. I became more and more nonresponsive and began to distance myself from my cooperating teacher. Rather than seeking assistance, I withdrew and neither asked questions nor made suggested changes.

At my midterm conference my university supervisor expressed concern that I did not appear committed to teaching. She said, "Rowan, you need to do more than just go through the motions because you are responsible for the learning of 75 students." At one point she hinted that I consider dropping out of the program if I did not have my heart in teaching and did not have the interest of the students as my priority. This conference was truly an eye-opener for me because dropping out would represent a first huge failure in my life. Thoughts of being a failure to myself, to my parents, to my grandmother scared me.

I resented my university supervisor's comments and told her that I've always finished what I started. Unfortunately my teaching didn't improve and my uneasiness turned into frustration once the papers to correct piled up. The amount of time I put into writing my detailed lesson plans aggravated my frustration. I was very overwhelmed as the suggestions to improve my teaching poured in from my cooperating teacher and my university supervisor. To relieve the pressure, I ignored their advice. Like an addictive drug, I continued to relieve my stress and avoid my problems in teaching by ignoring their suggestions.

At one point, my university supervisor suggested several interventions that required me to seriously reflect on my teaching. She required that I review my teaching videotape alone, and then view and discuss the videotape with her. As we collaboratively viewed the videotape, my perceptions of what was going on in the classroom were very narrow. When she tried to get me to discuss and explain what I thought was going on, I told her that I didn't respond to student cues because I wanted to accomplish my lesson objectives. I blamed the students for the problems in the lesson and said they were lazy and not motivated. I said that since they did not do their homework it was impossible for me to motivate the students. After reviewing the videotape, she asked me to watch it again and write up answers to a list of questions. (See videotape questions below.)

She also wanted me to visit and observe a cooperating teacher who had many of the same students in her class that I had in my class. My university supervisor wanted me to observe the teacher's instructional behaviors as well as observe my students' behaviors in the class. She gave me a list of specific teaching behaviors and strategies she wanted me to focus on during the observation. I was reluctant to observe the teacher because I heard she was a very nurturing teacher and the descriptions of her teaching from my peers contradicted my impartial, logi-

cal, and scientific teaching style. I visited the class only because my supervisor told me to do so. While I observed I was shocked to see my students behave so well in the class. This shocker led me to analyze the teacher's ability to soothe my students. Her teaching impressed me and I realized that my pre-conception of her was incomplete. She was nurturing, but she was also structured, and she clearly explained her expectations to her students. The teacher came up to me toward the end of class to provide her rationale of the lesson and what had been done to set the routines in her class. After this conversation as well as subsequent ones, I discovered that this teacher had become a "critical friend" to me. I realized from observing her teaching and talking with her, I had gained a different perspective on my students. I also found out that not all my beliefs or assumptions were correct or complete.

I consider my observations of this teacher to be the starting point of my growth because it catalyzed my willingness to accept suggestions that contradicted my beliefs and assumptions. I had evidence that contradicted my beliefs about my students being lazy, unmotivated, and in control of the class. These counterexamples to my beliefs and assumptions were critical in helping me reframe my thinking and my previous assumptions. Only when these observations challenged my previous beliefs was I ready to accept suggestions. I was beginning to see different perspectives and alternative explanations. My attitude and commitment began to shift.

In my fourth semester, I decided to critically reflect on my ups and downs and systematically study my teaching. I began to have discussions with my university supervisor about how I could go about studying my teaching. She gave me various articles to read about teacher beliefs and developmental stages of preservice teachers. Our conversations and the readings helped me to reflect on my experiences. As the reflections intensified, my paper evolved into thoroughly examining my student teaching experience and myself. I personalized my master's paper by looking at who I am and how it affected my student teaching. By reflecting, writing, and discussing my findings with my university supervisor, I revisited and reconstructed my experiences and began to come to a deeper understanding of myself as a person and as a teacher.

Method

Data for this study were collected over a period of two years. The data were derived from multiple sources including conversations, videotaped analyses of teaching, my cooperating teacher/student teacher dialogue journal, and individual assignments. The dialogue journal was maintained by the cooperating teacher, my university supervisor, and myself during my student teaching (third semester). Included in the entries were positive feedback, objective observational feedback, questions, and suggestions. The dialogue journal was intended to be interactive; however, I didn't write in it very often. The videotaped analyses were requirements in my third and fourth semesters. In addition to videotaping my teaching, I was required to write reflections of the videotaped lessons. Other sources of my data were my previous writings (e.g., philosophy of education and quarterly self-evaluations).

Data analysis

I read and reread my dialogue journal, reviewed the videotapes of my teaching, and reflected on assignments and conversations with my cooperating teacher and university supervisor. As I read the dialogue journal, I looked for recurring problems and possible themes. I used the constant comparison method of data analysis (Glaser & Strauss, 1967) to analyze the dialogue journal. In addition to the themes, I identified the context in which these themes occurred. I also analyzed two of my videotapes (one from the third semester and one from the fourth semester) to compare and contrast my teaching experiences. I analyzed the videotapes to

identify recurring themes. Tables were constructed which identified the themes, described the context, and analyzed the themes.

Findings

Dialogue journal

As mentioned earlier in this chapter, I analyzed the dialogue journal by reading through the comments over and over to discover recurring problems and to generalize the problems into themes. I identified the following recurring themes that emerged from the analysis of my third semester dialogue journal. The themes included

1 engagement;
2 structure;
3 consistency/follow through;
4 setting routines;
5 assessment;
6 instructional strategies; and
7 relationship to students' prior knowledge.

The analysis of the dialogue journal revealed the relationship of my instructional and management behaviors to the students' behaviors. The data suggest how the behavior of the teacher impacts the students' behavior. My analysis resulted in a shift in my thinking from the belief that the students control what is happening in the classroom to a heightened awareness of the impact of my actions on the students' attitudes and behavior. The complete analysis of the dialogue journal is shown in Table 2 in the previous section of this chapter which outlined the research process.

Videotape analysis

As you may recall from the earlier discussion of the videotape analysis, I used four of the themes that emerged from the analysis of the dialogue journal (engagement, structure, consistency/follow through, and setting routines) to systematically analyze two videotapes of my teaching. I analyzed a videotape from the third semester as well as one from the fourth semester. (See Tables 3 and 4 in the previous section for the analyses of the two videotapes.) I also examined how student engagement, structure, consistency/follow through, and routines impacted student behavior and learning. The analyses of the third and fourth semester videotapes provided a comparison and contrast of the changes I implemented in my teaching. In the fourth semester video analysis, I examined how specific instructional behaviors resulted in increased student engagement, time on task, and a focus on learning.

There is evidence that the instructional and management changes that I implemented in the fourth semester made a positive difference in the students' behavior and their learning. The findings show how I began to shift from a sense of helplessness to one of taking responsibility. My attitude shifted from blaming others to a willingness to critique and improve my teaching, and to focus on the students' learning as opposed to focusing on myself.

Evidence of Impact

In addition to the dialogue journal and the videotape analyses, I reread and analyzed many of my assignments and evaluations. I reflected on the obstacles I encountered during my preservice teaching. I realized that if I was going to understand myself as a teacher I needed to be honest when I reflected back on my professional journey. As I was writing my self-study, I met with my university supervisor and shared my data analysis and my reflections on my teaching experience. We discussed various critical incidents that occurred during my student teaching. Drawing upon the articles my university supervisor suggested and my notes from our collaborative discussions, I identified a number of themes that were obstacles to my growth as a teacher. The themes included, first of all, fear, second, responsibility, third, contradictions between my beliefs and practices, and, fourth closed-mindedness. I believe my

growth and development were negatively impacted by these different factors.

Fear

After one of my conversations with my university supervisor, I wrote that my fears were intertwined with feelings of blaming and anger and were fueled by my feelings of frustration and inadequacy. I wrote about my fear of idiocy and my fear of failure. I realized that as my fears increased, I became more stubborn. My fear of failure prevented me from confronting my problems and asking the cooperating teachers or colleagues for help. For me, denial and shutting down were defense mechanisms for having to face my worst fear, which was failing. I felt that if I ignored my cooperating teacher's and university supervisor's suggestions, it prevented me from failing. The threat of failing was a "wake up call" for me. It forced me to heed suggestions better and helped prepare me to observe the other cooperating teacher with an open eye. My visitation, my dialogue journal, and videotape analyses forced me to see contradictions in my beliefs and views about teaching.

Responsibility

I realized that it was easier for me to assign blame on others, rather than personally accept responsibility and possible failure. I did not incorporate suggestions because I felt that if the suggestions failed, that I would for sure have been a failure. I felt that I could avoid failure by ignoring feedback. Avoiding failure, to some extent, alleviated stress because it allowed me to mask any problems with my teaching.

Contradictions between my beliefs and my practice

In my philosophy of education I wrote that "learning takes place through hands-on experiences and other student-centered methods." I believed in involving students in group activities and labs. However, in reality, I lectured to my students because

I felt that lectures would be the only way my students would learn physics correctly. I did not trust my students to learn the "right" way if I permitted too much group work and other student-centered approaches. I realized that my thinking got in the way of my development. I came to realize that my teaching behaviors defaulted to the way I was taught and I was not open to taking risks. If I tried something and it did not go right, I abandoned it quickly and dismissed it as not effective.

Another realization I made through my self-study was that my cooperating teacher was there to help me, but I ignored his suggestions to improve my teaching. By ignoring my cooperating teacher, I failed to recognize that this was hurting my growth as a teacher. I even blamed him for my problems. I wrote that I was angry with him because I did not feel he was helping me at all. I saw him as the authority figure and could not identify with his collaborative, non-judgmental approach. I was not ready to accept him as a "critical friend." I wrote, "My intelligence also inhibited me to appreciate the teaching seminars, which were designed for the preservice teachers to learn from their peers and supervisors. I rarely participated in the seminar discussions because most of the resolutions to these discussions were common sense. I now realize the common sense of the seminars was not demonstrated by my teaching."

Reframing my thinking

During my student teaching, I was not aware of the obstacles and the contradictions between my beliefs and practice. My initial awareness came during my fourth semester when I began to gain confidence in myself, and was more willing to problem solve and search for ways to improve my teaching and my students' learning. I began to try out strategies from different teachers that were compatible with my beliefs and philosophy. I wanted to put my own personal identity into my teaching.

I gained valuable insight from conducting this

self-study of my teaching. If it were not for this paper, I would not have realized the full extent of the changes that occurred in my student teaching. As I reflected on and reconstructed my experiences, I began to come to a deeper understanding of myself as a person and as a teacher. By systematically analyzing the dialogue journal and my videotapes, I "scratched beneath the surface" and analyzed what I was doing and what impact it had on my students. An example of my self-awareness is revealed in the following quote from my master's paper: "The final and most important principle, reflection, demands that preservice teachers meta-cognitively think of why what happened." I realized that as I framed and reframed my thinking about teaching, I moved from the stance of being a student of teaching to being a teacher.

In the two years of the master's in teaching program, I had become accustomed to the principles of inquiry, collaboration, and reflection. Inquiry and collaboration were easy to get used to because these principles were similar to two collaborating scientists inquiring into the mysteries of physics. Reflection was a different story. It was only recently that I learned to appreciate the value and importance for a good teacher to reflect on himself or herself. Reflection was difficult for me because it did not conform to my scientific paradigm. Even though a physicist reflects on his or her experiment's effectiveness, he or she does not look at reflection with the same eyes as a teacher. This difference occurs because a teacher does not manipulate electrons or pi mesons, but works with ever-changing teens.

Although my journey from student to teacher was fraught with challenges and obstacles, I began to see myself differently as a result of my self-study. I began to shift my focus from myself to my students and came to a deeper understanding of the struggles and obstacles that are part of becoming a teacher. I discovered that the answers to handling difficult situations regarding how to teach could be found within myself. This paper forced me to open the

doors to the person I am. Even after writing this paper, I will leave the doors open so that I continue to grow and learn about myself.

Discussion

Now that you have read Rowan's formal self-study example, let's explore how his research qualifies as a self-study. Let's start by looking back to the methodological requirements and self-study dispositions we talked about in Chapter 4. His study included the requirements outlined by LaBoskey (2004b). The self-study was *self-initiated* and *improvement aimed*. Rowan started his inquiry with his personal concerns and a focus on himself and his teaching. He *systematically collected data* to examine his teaching and his students' learning with the goal of becoming a better teacher. His study involved *reflection* and *collaboration*. He reflected on his teaching individually and collaboratively by interacting with colleagues and the literature. Rowan engaged in *situated inquiry* as shown by the questions and concerns that arose from his own experiences and dilemmas. He used multiple sources of data and applied *qualitative research methods* to analyze his data. He shared his concerns and data with critical friends (a cooperating teacher and the university supervisor) to gain multiple perspectives.

As a result of his collaboration and systematic analysis of his data, Rowan *framed and reframed* his thinking about teaching and learning. He *formalized* his self-study by writing his master's paper and making it available to a wide audience. Ultimately, one of the most critical elements of the self-study process is that he transformed his thinking. Rowan grew personally and professionally as a result of his willingness to make himself vulnerable by critically and honestly examining his beliefs and actions. He made sense of his teaching by systematically reconstructing his experiences. His work makes a valuable contribution to our understanding of the highly complex and multidimensional process of becoming a teacher.

Questions for videotape analysis

1   Select three examples of direction-giving that occurred in the lesson. Explain why you selected these key examples and how you could improve on your directions and instructions. What could you have said to make things clearer for the students?

2   Select and analyze key incidents relating to classroom management. Indicate why you selected the key incidents and discuss what you could have done to improve classroom management. What specifically could you have said? What do you mean by needing their cooperation? What does this look like in terms of their behavior?

3   With regard to student understanding: Are there examples where you could help the students make connections across the activities you were doing? What about giving an overview of what they will be doing and why?

4   What are some of the students' questions that came up during the class? Write out examples of student questions. Explain what you did to address the questions. Please explain what you think was going on in the students' heads when they asked those questions. What might their questions tell you about their understanding or lack of understanding?

5   Did you give the students a sufficient overview of what you were going to do during your lesson? Would it be helpful for you to communicate to the students how you were going to help them fill out the form? Why or why not? Might it be helpful to tell them that you were going to go over each item one by one? Why or why not?

6   What kinds of questions did the students have in the previous class when you taught this lesson? What did you learn from the students' questions or behaviors in the previous class? What did you do differently as a result of the previous class?

7   How much time were students on task after you told them to collect their data toward the end

of class? Please give time in minutes.

8 Explain how what you do or not do in the class impacts student behaviors and student learning? What could you do differently in this particular lesson to positively change the students' behavior and learning?

9 Last part of the video—What could you have done differently? Be specific with regard to classroom management and student learning.

In Closing

We wrote this primer for you with the following five major goals. Our goals were to:

- present the definition and purposes of self-study
- provide an overview of the foundations of the self-study of teaching
- describe the nature of the self-study of teaching
- share guidelines for practicing the self-study of teaching methodology
- offer field-tested self-study methods with invitations to practice and examples of formal self-study research.

As inquiring professionals we reflect on our teaching. We make changes in our practice as we reframe our thinking based on our new insights. We share our insights to gain different perspectives. We try to make sense of our beliefs and our teaching practice in order to better understand ourselves and gain other perspectives. Self-study is a form of professional development that can lead to meaningful change as we better understand what we do, why we do it, and how we can improve our teaching. As active participants in our own inquiry we develop a sense of ownership as we identify and pose our own questions and dilemmas. We become actively engaged in constructing the knowledge individually and collaboratively. As we interact with others, we reframe and reconstruct our understandings with the aid of other perspectives and insights besides our own. We engage ourselves in critical reflection and inquiry, systematic data collection, data analysis, and collabo-

ration to gain multiple perspectives.

In this book we provided Invitations to Practice as practical activities to help you develop skills and habits of self-study. Our ultimate goal is for you to internalize a self-study stance toward your teaching and your students' learning.

Quickwrite

Now return to the quickwrite you wrote when you began reading this primer and consider what you have learned about self-study:

- What do you think of now when you hear the word "self-study of teaching?"
- How would you describe self-study?
- Who is involved in self-study?
- What purposes does self-study serve?
- How might you describe the nature of self-study?
- What are your goals for using self-study?

Implications of Self-Study

We close this book with four implications about the self-study of teaching. We ask you to consider which implications may be useful to you and your practice. We invite you to personally extend our list with your new understandings.

Self-study can make a difference in teachers' personal and professional development.

We believe that self-study methodology is essential to novice and experienced teachers as well as anyone else interested in examining and reframing their practice, regardless of discipline. Self-study embeds scholarship, ownership, and creativity into the hands of teachers as knowers and learners. We believe this is especially important within an aura of mandated test-driven teaching and within a time where teaching has become increasingly technical. It brings into focus the need for face-to-face dialogue with peers and colleagues to collectively work toward educational reform. Self-study of teaching practices begins to build the muscle for professional

development as a life-long process. It reminds us that some of the hardest and most important work is knowing oneself.

Teaching education programs can be enhanced with the inclusion of the self-study of teaching.

There are many innovations in teacher education programs (Cochran & Zeichner, 2005). We believe that seeking alternative ways of knowing, such as through self-study, can lead to further improvements. Self-study highlights the process of self-inquiry through our inter-action with others. Peers serve an important role in that process. As education students examine their teaching and try out their own innovations, they learn that without risk taking and trust there is no growth. Change is not linear in teacher education programs or in one's professional learning.

Self-study methodology has implications for how knowledge is defined, who defines it, where it is generated, and what individuals can contribute as knowers and doers in teacher reform efforts.

As a postmodern methodology, self-study stretches our way of thinking about how we know what we know. It also extends our way of thinking about the value of our ideas and actions and the essentialness of feedback from critical friends. Those outside per-spectives move us beyond our singular points of view and broaden our base of understanding our practice. Self-study places knowledge building in the hands of practitioners who see immediate results of their work as they examine their practice.

The Self-Study of Teaching SIG has demonstrated the influence of professional organizations in advancing the knowledge base of teaching and learning.

Self-study scholars have worked to model and bring the envisioning process for educational reform beyond the rhetoric to a reality where teachers work to reframe their own everyday teaching practices.

S-STEP has built a supportive and inclusive professional community for its members. The collaborative network and research have impacted teacher education programs, classrooms, and ultimately student learning and achievement. The ongoing work in self-study has made valuable contributions to the knowledge base of preservice and inservice teacher education. We are grateful to the community of scholars who have made our work possible.

Enjoy your self-study journey!

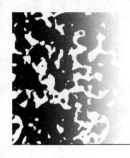

References & Resources

Allender, D. (2004). What happens to the self in self-study? In D. Tidwell, L. Fitzgerald, & M. Heston (Eds.), *Journeys of hope: Risking self-study in a diverse world.* Proceedings of the Fifth International Conference on Self-Study of Teacher Education Practices, Herstmonceux Castle, East Sussex, England (pp. 17–19). Cedar Falls, IA: University of Northern Iowa.

Allender, J. (2001). *Teacher self: The practice of humanistic education.* Lanham, MD: Rowman & Littlefield.

Allender, J., & Manke, M. P. (2004). Evoking self in self-study: The analysis of artifacts. In D. Tidwell, L. Fitzgerald, & M. Heston (Eds.), *Journeys of hope: Risking self-study in a diverse world.* Proceedings of the Fifth International Conference on Self-Study of Teacher Education Practices, Herstmonceux Castle, East Sussex, England (pp. 20–23). Cedar Falls, IA: University of Northern Iowa.

Austin, T., & Senese, J. C. (2004). Self-study in school teaching: Teachers' perspectives. In J. Loughran, M. L. Hamilton, V. K. LaBoskey, & T. Russell (Eds.), *International handbook of self-study of teaching and teacher education practices* (Vol. 2, pp. 1231–1258). Dordrecht: Kluwer Academic Publishers.

Barnes, D. (1998). Forward: Looking forward: The concluding remarks at the Castle Conference. In M. L. Hamilton, with S. Pinnegar, T. Russell, J. Loughran, & V. LaBoskey (Eds.), *Reconceptualizing teaching practice: Self-study in teacher education* (pp. ix–xiv). London: Falmer Press.

Bass, V., Anderson-Patton, V., & Allender, J. (2002). Self-study as a way of teaching and learning: A research collaborative re-analysis of self-study teaching portfolios. In J. J. Loughran & T. Russell (Eds.), *Improving teacher education practices through self-study* (pp. 56–69). London: Falmer Press.

Beck, C., Freese, A. R., & Kosnik, C. (2004). The preservice practicum: Learning through self-study in a professional setting. In J. J. Loughran, M. L. Hamilton, V. K. LaBoskey, & T. Russell (Eds.), *International handbook of self-study of teaching and teacher education practices* (Vol. 2, pp. 1259–1293). Dordrecht: Kluwer Academic Publishers.

Belenky, M. F., Clinchy, B. M., Goldberger, N. R., & Tarule, J. M. (1986). *Women's ways of knowing: The development of self, voice, and mind.* New York: Basic Books.

Ben-Peretz, M. (1995). *Learning from experience: Memory and the teacher's account of teaching.* Albany, NY: State University of New York Press.

Berry, A. (2004). Self-study in teaching about teaching. In J. J. Loughran, M. L. Hamilton, V. K. LaBoskey, & T. Russell (Eds.), *International handbook of self-study of teaching and teacher education practices* (Vol. 2, pp. 1295–1332). Dordrecht: Kluwer Academic Publishers.

Blumenthal, P. (1977, August). *A faculty self-study group approach to improving instruction quality.* Paper presented at the Annual Meeting of the American Psychological Association, San Francisco, California. (ERIC Document Reproduction Service No. ED 147715)

Bourdieu, P. (1990). *The logic of practice* (R. Nice, trans.) Stanford, CA: Stanford University Press.

Britzman, D. P. (1991). *Practice makes practice: A critical study of learning to teach.* Albany, NY: State University of New York Press.

Brown, A. (1994). The advancement of learning. *Educational Researcher, 23*(8), 4–12.

Brown, E. R. (2002). The (in)visibility of race in narrative constructions of the self. In J. J. Loughran & T. Russell (Eds.), *Improving teacher education practices through self-study* (pp. 145–160). London: Falmer Press.

Brown, J. S., Collins, A., & Duguid, P. (1989). Situated cognition and the culture of learning. *Educational Researcher, 18*(4), 32–42.

Bruner, J. (1990). *Acts of meaning*. Cambridge, MA: Harvard University Press.

Bullough, R. V., Jr., & Gitlin, A. (1995). *Becoming a student of teaching: Methodologies for exploring self and school context*. New York: Garland Publishers.

Bullough, R. V., Jr., & Pinnegar, S. (2001). Guidelines for quality in autobiographical forms of self-study research. *Educational Researcher, 30*(3), 13–21.

Bullough, R. V., Jr., & Pinnegar, S. (2004). Thinking about the thinking about self-study: An analysis of eight chapters. In J. J. Loughran, M. L. Hamilton, V. K. LaBoskey, & T. Russell (Eds.), *International handbook of self-study of teaching and teacher education practices* (Vol. 1, pp. 313–342). Dordrecht: Kluwer Academic Publishers.

Caine, R. N., & Caine, R. (1994). *Making connections: Teaching and the human brain*. Menlo Park, CA: Innovative Learning Publications.

Carr, W., & Kemmis, S. (1986). *Becoming critical: Education, knowledge and action research*. London: Falmer Press.

Clarke, A., & Erickson, G. (2004). The nature of teaching and learning in self-study. In J. J. Loughran, M. L. Hamilton, V. K. LaBoskey, & T. Russell (Eds.), *International handbook of self-study of teaching and teacher education practices* (Vol. 1, pp. 41–67). Dordrecht: Kluwer Academic Publishers.

Clift, R. T., Brady, P., Mora, R. A., Choi, S. J., & Stegemoller, J. (2006). From self-study to collaborative self-study to collaborative self-study of collaboration: Evolution of a research team. In C. Kosnik, C. Beck, A. R. Freese, & A. P. Samaras (Eds.), *Making a difference in teacher education through self-study: Studies of personal, professional, and program renewal* (pp. 85–100). Dordrecht: Springer.

Cochran-Smith, M., & Lytle, S. L. (1993). *Inside/Outside: Teacher research and knowledge*. New York: Teachers College Press.

Cochran-Smith, M., & Lytle, S. L. (2004). Practitioner inquiry, knowledge, and university culture. In J. J. Loughran, M. L. Hamilton, V. K. LaBoskey, & T. Russell (Eds.), *International handbook of self-study of teaching and teacher education practices* (Vol. 1, pp. 601–649). Dordrecht: Kluwer Academic Publishers.

Cochran-Smith, M., & Zeichner, K. (Eds.). (2005). *Studying teacher education: The Report of the AERA Panel on Research and Teacher Education.* Washington: American Educational Research Association/Lawrence Erlbaum.

Coia, L., & Taylor, M. (2004). What is at risk here? Recasting feminist authority through the lens of the past. In D. Tidwell, L. Fitzgerald, & M. Heston (Eds.), *Risking the journey of self-study in a diverse world.* Proceedings of the Fifth International Conference on Self-Study of Teacher Education Practices, Herstmonceux Castle, East Sussex, England (pp. 72–75). Cedar Falls, IA: University of Northern Iowa.

Cole, A. L., Elijah, R., & Knowles, J. G. (Eds.). (1998). *The heart of the matter: Teacher educators and teacher education reform.* San Francisco, CA: Caddo Gap Press.

Cole, A. L., & Finely, S. (Eds.). (1998). *Conversations in community.* Proceedings of the Second International Conference on Self-Study of Teacher Education Practices, Herstmonceux Castle, East Sussex, England. Kingston, ON: Queen's University.

Cole, A. L., & Knowles, J. G. (1996). The politics of epistemology and the self-study of teacher education practices. In J. Richards & T. Russell (Eds.), *Empowering our future in teacher education.* Proceedings of the First International Conference on the Self-Study of Teacher Education Practices, Herstmonceux Castle, East Sussex, England (pp. 67–73). Kingston, ON: Queen's University.

Cole, A. L., & Knowles, J. G. (1998). The self-study of teacher education practices and the reform of teacher education. In M. L. Hamilton, with S. Pinnegar, T. Russell, J. Loughran, & V. LaBoskey (Eds.), *Reconceptualizing teaching practice: Self-study in teacher education* (pp. 224–234). London: Falmer Press.

Cole, A. L., & Knowles, J. G. (2000). *Researching teaching: Exploring teacher development through reflexive inquiry.* Boston: Allyn and Bacon.

Colley, A. C. (2002). Teaching the Teachers, *Principal, 81*(4), 22–24.

Connelly, F. & Clandinin, D.J. (1990). Stories of experience and narrative inquiry. *Educational Researcher, 19*(5), 2–11.

Dana, N. F., & Yendal-Silva, D. (2003). *The reflective educator's guide to classroom research.* Thousand Oaks, CA. Corwin.

Darling-Hammond, L. (1997). *The right to learn: A blueprint for creating schools that work*. San Francisco: Jossey-Bass.

Dewey, J. (1916a). *Democracy and education*. New York: Macmillan.

Dewey, J. (1916b). *Essays in experimental logic*. Chicago: University of Chicago Press.

Dewey, J. (1933). *How we think: A restatement of the relation of reflective thinking to the reflective process*. New York: Heath and Company.

Dewey, J. (1938). *Experience and education*. New York: Macmillan.

Duckworth, J. (1987). *The having of wonderful ideas and other essays on teaching and learning*. New York: Teachers College Press.

Elijah, R. (2004). Voice in self-study. In J. J. Loughran, M. L. Hamilton, V. K. LaBoskey, & T. Russell (Eds.), *International handbook of self-study of teaching and teacher education practices* (Vol. 1, pp. 247–271). Dordrecht: Kluwer Academic Publishers.

Feldman, A. (2002). Bec(o/a)ming a teacher educator. In C. Kosnik, A. R. Freese, & A. P. Samaras (Eds.), *Making a difference in teacher education through self-study*. Proceedings of the Fourth International Conference on Self-Study of Teacher Education Practices, Herstmonceux Castle, East Sussex, England (Vol. 1, pp. 66–70). Toronto, ON: OISE, University of Toronto.

Feldman, A. (2003). Validity and quality in self-study. *Educational Researcher, 32*(3), 26–28.

Feldman, A. (2006). Using an existential form of reflection to understand my transformation as a teacher educator. In C. Kosnik, C. Beck, A. R. Freese, & A. P. Samaras (Eds.), *Making a difference in teacher education through self-study: Studies of personal, professional, and program renewal* (pp. 35–49). Dordrecht: Springer.

Feldman, A., Paugh, P., & Mills, G. (2004). Self-study through action research. In J. Loughran, M. L. Hamilton, V. K. LaBoskey, & J. Russell (Eds.), *International handbook of self-study of teaching and teacher education practices* (Vol. 2, pp. 943–977). Dordrecht: Kluwer Academic Publishers.

Fitzgerald, L. M., Farstad, J. E., & Deemer, D. (2002). What gets "mythed" in the student evaluations of their teacher education professors. In J. J. Loughran and T. Russell (Eds.), *Improving teacher education practices through self-study* (pp. 208–221). London: Routledge.

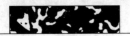

Fitzgerald, L., Heston, M., & Tidwell, D. (Eds.). (2006). *Collaboration and community: Pushing boundaries through self-study*. Proceedings of the Sixth International Conference on Self-Study of Teacher Education Practices, Herstmonceux Castle, East Sussex, England. Cedar Falls, IA: University of Northern Iowa.

Fosnot, C. (1989). *Enquiring teachers, enquiring learners: A constructivist approach for teaching*. New York: Teachers College Press.

Freese, A. R. (1999). The role of reflection on preservice teachers' development in the context of a professional development school. *Teaching and Teacher Education, 15*(8), 895–910.

Freese, A. R. (2002, April). *Reframing one's teaching: Discovering our teacher selves through reflection and inquiry*. Paper presented at the Annual Meeting of the American Educational Research Association Conference, New Orleans.

Freese, A. R. (2006). Transformation through self-study: The voices of preservice teachers. In C. Kosnik, C. Beck, A. R. Freese, & A. P. Samaras (Eds.), *Making a difference teacher education through self-study: Personal, professional, and program renewal* (pp. 65–79). Dordrecht: Springer.

Glaser, B. G., & Strauss, A. L. (1967). *The discovery of grounded theory*. Dallas: Houghton Mifflin.

Glaser, R. (1966, February). *The program for individually prescribed instruction*. (ERIC Document Reproduction Service No. ED 010519)

Guilfoyle, K. (1992, April). *Communicating with students: The impact of interactive dialogue journals on the thinking and teaching of a teacher educator*. Paper presented at the Annual Meeting of the American Education Research Association, San Francisco.

Guilfoyle, K., Hamilton, M. L., Pinnegar, S., & Placier, M. (1998). Negotiating balance between reforming teacher education and reforming self as teacher educators. In A. L. Cole, R. Elijah, & J. G. Knowles (Eds.), (pp. 171–192). *The heart of the matter: Teacher educators and teacher education reform*. San Francisco, CA: Caddo Gap Press.

Haberman, M. (1991). The pedagogy of poverty versus good teaching. *Phi Delta Kappan, 73*(3), 290–294.

Ham, V., & Davey, R. (2006). Is virtual teaching, real teaching? Learnings from two self-studies. In C. Kosnik, C. Beck, A. R. Freese, & A. P. Samaras (Eds.), *Making a dif-*

ference in teacher education through self-study: Studies of personal, professional, and program renewal (pp. 101–116). Dordrecht: Springer.

Ham, V., & Kane, R. (2004). Finding a way through the swamp: A case for self-study as research. In J. J. Loughran, M. L. Hamilton, V. K. LaBoskey, & T. Russell (Eds.), *International handbook of self-study of teaching and teacher education practices* (Vol. 1, pp. 103–150). Dordrecht: Kluwer Academic Publishers.

Hamilton, M. L. (1992, April). *Making public the private voice of a teacher educator.* Paper presented at the Annual Meeting of the American Education Research Association, San Francisco.

Hamilton, M. L. (2004). Professional knowledge and self-study teacher education. In J. J. Loughran, M. L. Hamilton, V. K. LaBoskey, & T. Russell (Eds.), *International handbook of self-study of teaching and teacher education practices* (Vol. 1, pp. 375–419). Dordrecht: Kluwer Academic Publishers.

Hamilton, M. L., & Pinnegar, S. (1998a. Conclusion. In M. L. Hamilton, S. Pinnegar, T. Russell, J. Loughran, & V. K. LaBoskey (Eds.), *Reconceptualizing teaching practice: Self-study in teacher education* (pp. 235–246). London: Falmer Press.

Hamilton, M. L., & Pinnegar, S. (1998b). Introduction. In M. L. Hamilton, S. Pinnegar, T. Russell. J. Loughran, & V. K. LaBoskey (Eds.), *Reconceptualizing teaching practice: Self-study in teacher education* (pp. 1–6). London: Falmer Press.

Hamilton, M. L., & Pinnegar, S. (1998c). Preface. In M. L. Hamilton, S. Pinnegar, T. Russell, J. Loughran, & V. K. LaBoskey (Eds.), *Reconceptualizing teaching practice: Self-study in teacher education* (p. viii). London: Falmer Press.

Hamilton, M. L., with Pinnegar, S., Russell, T., Loughran, J., & LaBoskey, V. (Eds.). (1998). *Reconceptualizing teaching practice: Self-study in teacher education.* London: Falmer Press.

Hamilton, M. L., & Pinnegar, S. (2000). On the threshold of a new century: Trustworthiness, integrity, and self-study in teacher education. *Journal of Teacher Education, 51*(3), 234–240.

Hawley, W. D., & Valli, L. (1999). The essentials of effective professional development. In L. Darling-Hammond & G. Sykes (Eds.), *Teaching as the learning profession: Handbook of policy and practice* (pp. 127–150). San

Francisco: Jossey-Bass.

Hoban, G. F. (2004). Using information and communication technologies for the self-study of teaching. In J. J. Loughran, M. L. Hamilton, V. K. LaBoskey, & T. Russell (Eds.), *International handbook of self-study of teaching and teacher education practices* (Vol. 2, pp. 1039–1072). Dordrecht: Kluwer Academic Publishers.

Holzman, L. (1997). *Schools for growth: Radical alternatives to current educational methods*. Mahwah, NJ: Lawrence Erlbaum.

Hubbard, R. S., & Power, B. M. (1999). *The art of classroom inquiry: A handbook for teacher-researchers*. Portsmouth, NH: Heinemann.

Ingersoll, R. (2001). Teacher turnover and teacher shortages: An organizational analysis. *American Educational Research Journal, 38*(3), 499–534.

Kelchtermans, G., & Hamilton, M. L. (2004). The dialectics of passion and theory: Exploring the relation between self-study and emotion. In J. J. Loughran, M. L. Hamilton, V. K. LaBoskey, & T. Russell (Eds.), *International handbook of self-study of teaching and teacher education practices* (Vol. 1, pp. 785–810). Dordrecht: Kluwer Academic Publishers.

Kincheloe, J. K. (1991). *Teachers as researchers: Qualitative inquiry as a path to empowerment*. London: Falmer Press.

Knowles, J. G. (1970). *The modern practice of adult education: Andragogy versus pedagogy*. New York: Association Press.

Knowles, J. G., & Cole, A. L. (1991). *We're just like those we study—They as beginning teachers, we as beginning professors of teacher education: Letters of the first year*. Paper presented at the Bergamo Conference on Curriculum Theory and Classroom Practice in Dayton, Ohio.

Knowles, J. G., & Cole, A. L. (1994). We're just like those we study: Letters and reflections on our first year as beginning professors. *Curriculum Inquiry, 24*(1), 27–54.

Knowles, J. G., & Cole, A. L., with Presswood, C. S. (1994). *Through preservice teachers' eyes: Exploring field experiences through narrative and inquiry*. New York: Merrill/Macmillan.

Korthagen, F.A.J. (1995). A reflection on five reflective accounts. Theme issue self study and living educational theory. *Teacher Educational Quarterly, 22*(3), 99–105.

Kosnik, C. (1998). Conflicting and competing agendas: A

school-university partnership. In A. L. Cole, R. Elijah, & J. G. Knowles (Eds.), *The heart of the matter: Teacher educators and teacher education reform* (pp. 193–210). San Francisco, CA: Caddo Gap Press.

Kosnik, C., Beck, C., & Freese, A. R. (2004). The preservice practicum: Learning through self-study in a professional setting. In J. J. Loughran, M. L. Hamilton, V. K. LaBoskey, & T. Russell (Eds.), *International handbook of self-study of teaching and teacher education practices* (Vol. 2, pp. 1259–1293). Dordrecht: Kluwer Academic Publishers.

Kosnik, C., & Beck, C. (2006). The impact of a preservice teacher education program on language arts teaching practices: A study of second-year teachers. In C. Kosnik, C. Beck, A. R. Freese, & A. P. Samaras (Eds.), *Making a difference in teacher education through self-study: Studies of personal, professional, and program renewal* (pp. 243–259). Dordrecht: Springer.

Kosnik, C., Freese, A. R., & Samaras, A. P. (Eds.). (2002). *Making a difference in teacher education through self-study.* Proceedings of the Fourth International Conference on Self-Study of Teacher Education Practices, Herstmonceux Castle, East Sussex, England (Vols. 1 & 2). Toronto, ON: OISE, University of Toronto.

Kosnik, C., Beck, C., Freese, A. R., & Samaras, A. P. (Eds.). (2006). *Making a difference in teacher education through self-study: Studies of personal, professional, and program renewal.* Dordrecht: Springer.

Kosnik, C., Samaras, A. P., & Freese, A. R. (2006). Beginning with trusted friends: Venturing out to work collaboratively in our institutions. In L. Fitzgerald, M. Heston, & D. Tidwell, (Eds.), *Collaboration and community: Pushing boundaries through self-study.* Proceedings of the Sixth International Conference on Self-Study of Teacher Education Practices, Herstmonceux Castle, East Sussex, England. Cedar Falls, IA: University of Northern Iowa.

Kuhn, T. (1970). *The structure of scientific revolutions.* Chicago: University of Chicago Press.

LaBoskey, V. K. (1994). *Development of reflective practice.* New York: Teachers College Press.

LaBoskey, V. K. (2004a). Afterword: Moving the methods of self-study research and practice forward: Challenges and opportunities. In J. J. Loughran, M. L. Hamilton, V. K. LaBoskey, & T. Russell (Eds.), *International handbook of self-study of teaching and teacher education prac-*

tices (Vol. 2, pp. 1169–1184). Dordrecht: Kluwer Academic Publishers.

LaBoskey, V. K. (2004b). The methodology of self-study and its theoretical underpinnings. In J. J. Loughran, M. L. Hamilton, V. K. LaBoskey, & T. Russell (Eds.), *International handbook of self-study of teaching and teacher education practices* (Vol. 1, pp. 817–869). Dordrecht: Kluwer Academic Publishers.

Lawrence-Lightfoot, S. (1983). *The good high school: Portraits of character and culture.* New York: Basic Books, Inc.

Lighthall, F. F. (2004). Fundamental features and approaches of the s-step enterprise. In J. J. Loughran, M. L. Hamilton, V. K. LaBoskey, & T. Russell (Eds.), *International handbook of self-study of teaching and teacher education practices* (Vol. 1, pp. 193–245). Dordrecht: Kluwer Academic Publishers.

Loughran, J. J. (1996). *Developing the reflective practitioner: Learning about teaching and learning through modeling.* London: Falmer Press.

Loughran, J. J. (2004). A history and context of self-study of teaching and teacher education practices. In J. J. Loughran, M. L. Hamilton, V. K. LaBoskey, & T. Russell (Eds.), *International handbook of self-study of teaching and teacher education practices* (Vol. 1, pp. 7–39). Dordrecht: Kluwer Academic Publishers.

Loughran, J. J. (2005). Researching teaching about teaching: Self-study of teacher education practices. *Studying Teacher Education, 1*(1), 5–16.

Loughran, J. J., Hamilton, M. L., LaBoskey, V. K., & Russell, T. (Eds.). (2004). *International handbook of self-study of teaching and teacher education practices.* Dordrecht: Kluwer Academic Publishers.

Loughran, J. J., & Northfield, J. (1998). A framework for the development of self-study practice. In M. L. Hamilton, with S. Pinnegar, T. Russell, J. Loughran, & V. K. LaBoskey (Eds.), *Reconceptualizing teaching practice: Self-study in teacher education* (pp. 7–18). London: Falmer Press.

Loughran, J. J., & Russell, T. (1997). *Teaching about teaching: Purpose, passion, and pedagogy in teacher education.* London: Falmer Press.

Loughran, J. J., & Russell, T. (Eds.). (2000). *Exploring myths and legends of teacher education.* Proceedings of the Third International Conference on the Self-Study of Teacher Education Practices, Herstmonceux Castle, East Sussex, England. Kingston, ON: Queen's University.

Loughran, J. J., & Russell, T. (2002). *Improving teacher education practices through self-study*. London: Routledge/Falmer.

Lyons, N., & Freidus, H. (2004). The reflective portfolio in self-study: Inquiring into and representing a knowledge about practice. In J. J. Loughran, M. L. Hamilton, V. K. LaBoskey, & T. Russell (Eds.), *International handbook of self-study of teaching and teacher education practices* (Vol. 2, pp. 1073–1107). Dordrecht: Kluwer Academic Publishers.

Manke, M. P. (2004). Administrators also do self-study: Issues of power and community, social justice, and teacher education reform. In J. J. Loughran, M. L. Hamilton, V. K. LaBoskey, & T. Russell (Eds.), *International handbook of self-study of teaching and teacher education practices* (Vol. 2, pp.1367–1391). Dordrecht: Kluwer Academic Publishers.

McNiff, J. (1988). *Action research: Principles and practice*. London: Routledge Press.

McNiff, J., Lomax, P., & Whitehead, J. (2004). *You and your action research project*. London: Routledge/Falmer.

McVarish, J., & Rust, F. (2006). Unsquaring teacher education. In C. Kosnik, C. Beck, A. R. Freese, & A. P. Samaras (Eds.), *Making a difference in teacher education through self-study: Studies of personal, professional, and program renewal* (pp. 185–201). Dordrecht: Springer.

Mills, G. (2000). *Action research: A guide for the teacher researchers*. Upper Saddle River, NJ: Merrill.

Mills, G. (2003). *Action research: A guide for the teacher researchers* (2nd ed.). Upper Saddle River, NJ: Merrill Prentice Hall.

Mitchell, C. (2006). In my own handwriting: Textual evidence and self-study. In C. Kosnik, C. Beck, A. R. Freese, & A. P. Samaras (Eds.), *Making a difference in teacher education through self-study: Studies of personal, professional, and program renewal* (pp. 117–130). Dordrecht: Springer.

Mitchell, C., & Weber, S. (1998). Picture this! Class-line ups, vernacular portraits and lasting impressions. In J. Prosser (Ed.), *Image-based research: A sourcebook for qualitative researchers* (pp. 197–213). London & Bristol: Falmer Press.

Mitchell, C., & Weber, S. (1999). *Reinventing ourselves as teachers: Beyond nostalgia*. London: Falmer Press.

Munby, H. (1996). Being taught by my teaching: Self study

in the realm of education computing. In J. Richards & T. Russell (Eds.), *Empowering our future in teacher education*. Proceedings of the First International Conference on the Self-Study of Teacher Education Practices, Herstmonceux Castle, East Sussex, England (pp. 62–66). Kingston, ON: Queen's University.

Munby, H., & Russell, T. (1990). Metaphor in the study of teachers' professional knowledge. *Theory into Practice, 29*(2), 116–121.

National Center for Educational Statistics. Retrieved July 9, 2005 from http://nces.ed.gov/.

Newman, F., & Holzman, L. (1993). *Lev Vygotsky: Revolutionary scientist*. London: Routledge.

Novak, J., & Gowin, D. (1984). *Learning how to learn*. New York: Cambridge University Press.

O'Reilly-Scanlon, K. (2002). Muted echoes and lavender shadows: Memory work and self-study. In C. Kosnik, A. R. Freese, & A. P. Samaras (Eds.), *Making a difference in teacher education through self-study*. Proceedings of the Fourth International Conference on Self-Study of Teacher Education Practices, Herstmonceux Castle, East Sussex, England (Vol. 2, pp. 74–78). Toronto, ON: OISE, University of Toronto.

Pinnegar, S. (1992, April). *Student teaching as a teacher educator*. Paper presented at the Annual Meeting of the American Education Research Association, San Francisco.

Pinnegar, S. (1998). Introduction: Methodological perspectives. In M. L. Hamilton, with S. Pinnegar, T. Russell, J. Loughran, & V. LaBoskey (Eds.), *Reconceptualizing teaching practice: Self-study in teacher education* (pp. 31-33). London: Falmer Press.

Placier, P. (1992, April). *Maintaining practice: A struggle of too little time*. Paper presented at the Annual Meeting of the American Education Research Association, San Francisco.

Richards, J. C. (1998). Turning to the artistic: Developing an enlightened eye by creating teaching self-portraits. In M. L. Hamilton, with S. Pinnegar, T. Russell, J. Loughran, & V. LaBoskey (Eds.), *Reconceptualizing teacher practice: Self-study in teacher education* (pp. 34–44). London: Falmer Press.

Richards, J., & Russell, T. (Eds.). (1996). *Empowering our future in teacher education*. Proceedings of the First International Conference on Self-Study of Teacher

Education Practices, Herstmonceux Castle, East Sussex, England. Kingston, ON: Queen's University.

Richardson, V. (1989). The evolution of reflective teaching and teacher education. In R. Clift, W.R. Houston, & M. Pugach, *Encouraging reflective practice: An examination of issues and exemplars* (pp. 3–19). New York: Teachers College Press.

Robinson, V. (1993). *Problem-based methodology: Research for the improvement of practice.* Oxford: Pergamon.

Russell, T. (1987). Research, practical knowledge and the conduct of teacher education. *Educational Theory, 37*(4), 369–375.

Russell, T. (1992, April). Holding up the mirror: A teacher educator and his students reflect on teaching high school physics. Paper presented at the Annual Meeting of the American Education Research Association. San Francisco.

Russell, T. (1998). Philosophical perspectives. Introduction. In M. L. Hamilton, with S. Pinnegar, T. Russell, J. Loughran, & V. LaBoskey (Eds.), *Reconceptualizing teaching practice: Self-study in teacher education* (pp. 5–6). London: Falmer Press.

Russell, T. (2002). Can self-study improve teacher education? In J. J. Loughran & T. Russell (Eds.), *Improving teacher education practices through self-study* (pp. 3–10). London: Routledge/Falmer.

Russell, T. (2006). How 20 years of self-study changed my teaching. In C. Kosnik, C. Beck, A. R. Freese, & A. P. Samaras (Eds.), *Making a difference in teacher education through self-study: Studies of personal, professional, and program renewal* (pp. 3–17). Dordrecht: Springer.

Russell, T., & Korthagen, F. (1995). *Teachers who teach teachers: Reflections on teacher education.* London: Falmer Press.

Russell, T., & Munby, H. (Eds.). (1992). *Teachers and teaching: From classroom to reflection.* London: Falmer Press.

Samaras, A. P. (1991). Transitions to competence: An investigation of adult mediation in preschoolers' self-regulation with a microcomputer-based problem-solving task. *Early Education and Development, 2*(3), 181–196.

Samaras, A. P. (1995). My journey to Ithaca: Reflections of a teacher educator. *Teaching Education, 7*(1), 96–101.

Samaras, A. P. (1998). Finding my way: Teaching methods

courses from a sociocultural perspective. In A. L. Cole, R. Elijah, & J. G. Knowles (Eds.), *The heart of the matter: Teacher educators and teacher education reform* (pp. 55–79). San Francisco, CA: Caddo Gap Press.

Samaras, A. P. (2000). When is a practicum productive? A study in learning to plan. *Action in Teacher Education, 22*(2), 100–112.

Samaras, A. P. (2002). *Self-study for teacher educators: Crafting a pedagogy for educational change.* New York: Peter Lang.

Samaras, A. P., Beck, A., Freese, A. R., & Kosnik, C. (2005). Self-study supports new teachers' professional development. *Focus on Teacher Education Quarterly, 6(1),* 3–5 & 7.

Samaras, A. P., DeMulder, E. K., Kayler, M. A., Newton, L., Rigsby, L. C., Weller, K. L., & Wilcox, D. R. (2006). Spheres of learning in teacher collaboration. In C. Kosnik, C. Beck, A. R. Freese, & A. P. Samaras (Eds.), *Making a difference in teacher education through self-study: Studies of personal, professional, and program renewal* (pp. 147–163). Dordrecht: Springer.

Samaras, A. P., & Gismondi, S. (1998). Scaffolds in the field: Vygotskian interpretation in a teacher education program. *Teaching and Teacher Education, 14,* 715–733.

Samaras, A. P., Hicks, M. A., & Berger, J. G. (2004). Self-study through personal history. In J. J. Loughran, M. L. Hamilton, V. K. LaBoskey, & T. Russell (Eds.), *International handbook of self-study of teaching and teacher education practices* (Vol. 2, pp. 905–942). Dordrecht: Kluwer Academic Publishers.

Samaras, A. P., Kayler, M. A., Rigsby, L. C., Weller, K. L., & Wilcox, D. R. (2006). Self-study of the craft of faculty team teaching in a non-traditional teacher education program. *Studying Teacher Education, 2*(1), 43–57.

Samaras, A. P., & with contributions by Reed, R. L. (2000). Transcending traditional boundaries through drama: Interdisciplinary teaching and perspective-taking. In J. Loughran & T. Russell (Eds.), *Exploring myths and legends of teacher education.* Proceedings of the Third International Conference on Self-Study of Teacher Education Practices, Herstmonceux Castle, East Sussex, England (pp. 218–222). Kingston, ON: Queen's University.

Schön, D. A. (1983). *The reflective practitioner: How professionals think in action.* New York: Basic Books.

Schön, D. A. (1987). *Educating the reflective practitioner:*

Toward a new design for teaching and learning in the profession. San Francisco, CA: Jossey-Bass.

Schwab, J. J. (1973). The practical 3: Translation into curriculum. *School Review, 81*(4), 501–522.

Senese, J. (2002). Opposites attract: What I learned about being a classroom teacher by being a teacher educator. In J. J. Loughran & T. Russell (Eds.), *Improving teacher education practices through self-study* (pp. 43–55). London: Routledge/Falmer.

Smith, H. A. (1998). Self-study and the development of collective knowledge. In M. L. Hamilton, with S. Pinnegar, T. Russell, J. Loughran, & V. LaBoskey (Eds.), *Reconceptualizing teaching practice: Self-study in teacher education* (pp. 19–29). London: Falmer Press.

Tidwell, D. (2002). A balancing act: Self-study in valuing the individual student. In J. J. Loughran & T. Russell (Eds.), *Improving teacher education practices through self-study* (pp. 30–42). London: Routledge/Falmer.

Tidwell, D., Fitzgerald, L., & Heston, M. (Eds.). (2004). *Risking the journey of self-study in a diverse world.* Proceedings of the Fifth International Conference on Self-Study of Teacher Education Practices, Herstmonceux Castle, East Sussex, England. Cedar Falls, IA: University of Northern Iowa.

Trumbull, D. (1990). Evolving conceptions of teaching: reflections of one teacher. *Curriculum Inquiry, 20*(2), 161–182.

Trumbull, D. (2004). Factors important for the scholarship of self-study of teaching and teacher education practices. In J. J. Loughran, M. L. Hamilton, V. K. LaBoskey, & T. Russell (Eds.), *International handbook of self-study of teaching and teacher education practices* (Vol. 2, pp. 1211–1230). Dordrecht: Kluwer Academic Publishers.

Upitis, R., & Russell, T. (1998). Building a teacher education community: Combining electric mail with face-to-face interactions. In M. L. Hamilton, S. Pinnegar, T. Russell, J. Loughran, & V. LaBoskey (Eds.), *Reconceptualizing teaching practice: Self-study in teacher education* (pp. 77–109). London: Falmer Press.

Vygotsky, L. S. (1978). *Mind in society: The development of higher psychological processes.* In M. Cole, V. John-Steiner, S. S. Scribner, & E. Souberman (Eds.), Cambridge, MA: Harvard University Press.

Vygotsky, L. S. (1981). The genesis of higher mental func-

tions. In J. V. Wertsch (Ed.), *The concept of activity in Soviet psychology* (pp. 144–188). Armonk, NY: Sharpe. [Original work published 1960]

Weber, S., & Mitchell, C. (1996). Drawing ourselves into teaching: Studying the images that shape and distort teacher education. *Teaching & Teacher Education, 12*(3), 303–313.

Weber, S., & Mitchell, C. (2002). Academic literacy performance, embodiment, and self-study: When the shoe doesn't fit: Death of a salesman. In C. Kosnik, A. R. Freese, & A. P. Samaras (Eds.), *Making a difference in teacher education through self-study.* Proceedings of the Fourth International Conference on Self-Study of Teacher Education Practices, Herstmonceux Castle, East Sussex, England (Vol. 2, pp. 121–124). Toronto, ON: OISE, University of Toronto.

Whitehead, J. (1989). Creating a living educational theory from questions of the kind, 'How do I improve my practice?' *Cambridge Journal of Education, 19*(1), 41–52.

Whitehead, J. (1993). *The growth of educational knowledge: Creating your own living educational theories.* Bournemouth: Hyde Productions.

Whitehead, J. (2004). What counts as evidence in self-studies of teacher education practices? In J. J. Loughran, M. L. Hamilton, V. K. LaBoskey, & T. Russell (Eds.), *International handbook of self-study of teaching and teacher education practices* (Vol. 2, pp. 871–903). Dordrecht: Kluwer Academic Publishers.

Wilcox, S., Watson, J., & Paterson, M. (2004). Self-study in professional practice. In J. J. Loughran, M. L. Hamilton, V. K. LaBoskey, & T. Russell (Eds.), *International handbook of self-study of teaching and teacher education practices* (Vol. 1, pp. 273–312). Dordrecht: Kluwer Academic Publishers.

Zeichner, K. M. (1996). Teachers as reflective practitioners and the democratization of school reform. In K. Zeichner, S. Melnick, & M. L. Gomez (Eds.), *Currents of reform in preservice teacher education* (pp. 199–214). New York: Teachers College Press.

Zeichner, K. M. (1999). The new scholarship in teacher education. *Educational Researcher, 28*(9), 4–15.

Zeichner, K. M., & Liston, D. P. (1987). Teaching student teachers to reflect. *Harvard Educational Review, 57*(1), 23–48.

Zeichner, K. M., & Liston, D. P. (1996).*Reflective teaching: An introduction.* Mahwah, NJ: Lawrence Erlbaum.

Resources

Resource A

Comprehensive References

Loughran, J. J., Hamilton, M. L., LaBoskey, V. K., & Russell, T. (Eds.). (2004). *The International handbook of self-study of teaching and teacher education practices*. Dordrecht: Kluwer Academic Publishers.

According to the Web page, *The International Handbook on Self-study of Teaching and Teacher Education Practices* "is of interest to teacher educators, teacher researchers and practitioner researchers. [The handbook] offers an encyclopedic review of the field of self-study; examines in detail self-study in a range of teaching and teacher education contexts; outlines a full understanding of the nature and development of self-study; explores the development of a professional knowledge base for teaching through self-study; purposefully represents self-study through research and practice; illustrates examples of self-study in teaching and teacher education. Written for: Teacher educators, teacher researchers, practitioner researchers."

Web site: http://www.wkap.nl/prod/b/1–4020–1812–6 *Studying Teacher Education:* A journal of self-study of teacher education practices. According to the Web page, *Studying Teacher Education* "is an internationally refereed journal that welcomes papers from authors who have an interest in research and practice in teaching and teacher education. The main purpose of the journal is to foster research and dialogue in the study of teaching and teacher education practices, with a view to encouraging and widely disseminating such research and dialogue. In so doing, the journal is a forum for educators who work in a wide variety of settings and who are seeking to make substantial contributions to:

- self-study research, design, and practice
- the knowledge base of teaching and teaching about teaching
- enhanced understandings of learning to teach
- the nature of teacher education
- the professional development of teachers and teacher educators.

The journal seeks to create opportunities for teachers and teacher educators to publish empirical and conceptual research that advances our understanding of the complex work of teaching and teacher education."

Web site: http://www.tandf.co.uk/journals/titles/17425964.asp
Editors' Web page: http://post.queensu.ca/~ste/

Cochran-Smith, M., & Zeichner, K. M. (Eds.). (2005). *Studying Teacher Education: The Report of the AERA Panel on Research and Teacher Education.* Washington: American Educational Research Association/Lawrence Erlbaum.

A comprehensive analysis and review of research on teacher education and proposes a research agenda on teacher education for the future.

Resource B

Collection of Self-Study Related Books

Allender, S. (2001). *Teacher self: The practice of humanistic education.* Lanham, MD: Rowman & Littlefield Publishers.

Aubusson, P., & Schuck, S. (2006). *Teacher learning and development: The Mirror maze.* Dordrecht: Kluwer/Springer

Bullough, R. V., Jr. & Gitlin, A. (1995). *Becoming a student of teaching: Methodologies for exploring self and school context.* New York: Garland Publishers.

Cole, A. L., Elijah, R., & Knowles, J. G. (Eds.). (1998). *The heart of the matter: Teacher educators and teacher education reform.* San Francisco, CA: Caddo Gap Press.

Cole, A. L., & Knowles, J. G. (2000). *Researching teaching: Exploring teacher development through reflexive inquiry.* Boston: Allyn and Bacon.

Hamilton, M. L., with Pinnegar, S., Russell, T. Loughran, J. J., & LaBoskey, V. (Eds.). (1998). *Reconceptualizing teaching practice: Self-study in teacher education.* London: Falmer.

Hoban, G. F. (Ed.) (2005). *The missing links in teacher education design.* Dordrecht: Kluwer Academic Publishers.

Knowles, J. G., & Cole, A. L., with Presswood, C. S. (1994). *Through preservice teachers' eyes: Exploring field experiences through narrative and inquiry.* New York: Merrill/Macmillan.

Kosnik, C., Beck, C., Freese, A. R., & Samaras, A. P. (Eds.).

(2006). *Making a difference in teacher education through self-study: Studies of personal, professional, and program renewal*. Dordrecht: Springer.

Loughran, J. J. (1996). *Developing reflective practitioners: Learning about teaching and learning through modeling*. London: Falmer Press.

Loughran, J. J. (2006). *Developing a pedagogy of teacher education: Understanding teaching and learning about teaching*. London: Routledge.

Loughran, J. J., Hamilton, M. L., LaBoskey, V. K., & Russell, T. (Eds.). (2004). *International handbook of self-study of teaching and teacher education practices*. Dordrecht: Kluwer Academic Publishers.

Loughran, J. J., Mitchell, I. J., & Mitchell, J. (Eds.). (2002). *Learning from teacher Research*. New York: Teachers College Press.

Loughran, J. J., & Northfield, J.R. (1996). *Opening the classroom door: Teacher, researcher, learner*. London: Falmer Press.

Loughran, J. J., & Russell, T. (1997). *Teaching about teaching: Purpose, passion, and pedagogy in teacher education*. London: Falmer Press.

Loughran, J. J., & Russell, T. (Eds.). (2002) *Improving teacher education practices through self-study*. London: Routledge/Falmer.

Lyons, N., LaBoskey, V. K. (2002). *Narrative inquiry in practice: Advancing the knowledge of teaching*. New York: Teachers College Press.

McNiff, J., Lomax, P., & Whitehead, J. (2004). *You and your action research project*. London: Routledge/Falmer.

Mitchell, C., Weber, S. (1995). *That's funny, you don't look like a teacher! Interrogating images and identify in popular culture*. London: Falmer Press.

Mitchell, C., & Weber, S. (1999). *Reinventing ourselves as teachers: Beyond nostalgia*. London: Falmer Press.

Mitchell, C., Weber, S., & O'Reilly-Scanlon, K. (2005). *Just who do we think we are? Methodologies for autobiography and self-study*. London: Routledge/Falmer.

Muchmore, J. A. (2004). *A teacher's life: Stories of literacy, teacher thinking, and professional development*. San Francisco: Caddo Gap Press, & Halifax, NS: Backalong Books.

Russell, T., & Korthagen, F. (1995). *Teachers who teach teachers: Reflections on teacher education*. London: Falmer

Press.

Samaras, A. P. (2002). *Self-study for teacher educators: Crafting a pedagogy for educational change.* New York: Peter Lang.

Samaras, A. P., & Freese, A. R. (2006). *Self-study of teaching practices primer.* New York: Peter Lang.

SooHoo, S. (2006). *Talking leaves: Narratives of otherness.* Cresskill, NJ: Hampton Press.

Tidwell, D., & Fitzgerald, L. M. (Eds.). (2006). *Self-study and diversity.* Rotterdam, The Netherlands: Sense Publishers.

Weber, S., & Mitchell, M. (Eds.). (2004). *Not just any dress: Narratives of memory, body, and identity.* New York: Peter Lang.

Whitehead, J. (1993). *The growth of educational knowledge: Creating your own living educational theories.* Bournemouth: Hyde Productions.

Resource C

Collection of Self-Study Publications Organized by Topic

We invited our self-study colleagues to assist us in identifying self-study publications by topic areas so we could make them easily accessible to your research interests. We gleaned the topics from our literature review and asked authors to select the topic that best fits their publication. Below is just a sampling of self-study publications organized by topic to get you started in your further self-study research. You will note that some publications may relate to more than one area, e.g., an arts-based study with preservice teachers dealing with diversity and women. The papers from the Castle Conferences are available online. (See the Web sites listed in Resource F: The Castle Conferences.)

Topics

Arts-Based Self-Study • Classroom Teachers • Educational reform/leadership • Intersections among self-study/teacher/learner • Methodology • Preservice Teachers • Processes of Self-Study •Professional Development • Social Justice/Diversity • Technology

Arts-Based Self-Study

Allender, J., & Manke, M. P. (2004). Evoking self in self-study: The analysis of artifacts. In D. Tidwell, L. Fitzgerald, & M. Heston (Eds.), *Journeys of hope: Risking self-study in a diverse world*. Proceedings of the Fifth International Conference on Self-Study of Teacher Education Practices, Herstmonceux Castle, East Sussex, England (pp. 20–23).Cedar Falls, IA: University of Northern Iowa.

Butler-Kisber, L. (2005). Inquiry through poetry: The genesis of self-study. In C. Mitchell, S. Weber, & K. O'Reilly-Scanlon (Eds.), *Just who do we think we are? Methodologies for autobiography and self-study in teaching* (pp. 95–110). London: Routledge/Falmer.

Derry, C. (2005). Drawings as a research tool for self-study: An embodied method of exploring memories of childhood bullying. In C. Mitchell, S. Weber, & K. O'Reilly-Scanlon (Eds.), *Just who do we think we are? Methodologies for autobiography and self-study in teaching* (pp. 34–46). London: Routledge/Falmer.

Griffiths, M., Windle, J., & Simms, M. (2004). Academic and support staff: Images of three working lives in teacher education. In D. Tidwell, L. Fitzgerald, & M. Heston (Eds.), *Risking the journey of self-study in a diverse world*. Proceedings of the Fifth International Conference on Self-Study of Teacher Education Practices, Herstmonceux Castle, East Sussex, England (pp. 270–272). Cedar Falls, IA: University of Northern Iowa.

Mitchell, C., & Weber, S. J. (1996). He draws/she draws: Texts of interrogation. *Textual Studies of Canada: Canadian Journal of Cultural Literacy, 7*, 133–142.

Mitchell, C., & Weber, S. J. (1998). Picture this! Class-line ups, vernacular portraits and lasting impressions. In J. Prosser (Ed.), *Image-based research. A sourcebook for qualitative researchers* (pp. 197–213). London & Bristol: Falmer Press.

Mitchell, C., & Weber, S. (1998). The usable past: Teacher (re)playing school. *Changing English, 5*(1), 45–56.

Mitchell, C., & Weber, S. (1999). *Reinventing ourselves as teachers: Beyond nostalgia*. London: Falmer Press.

O'Reilly-Scanlon, K. (2002). Muted echoes and lavender shadows: Memory work and self-study. In C. Kosnik, A. R. Freese, & A. P. Samaras (Eds.), *Making a difference in teacher education through self-study*. Proceedings of the Fourth International Conference on Self-Study of

Teacher Education Practices, Herstmonceux Castle, East Sussex, England (Vol. 2, pp. 74–78). Toronto, ON: OISE, University of Toronto.

Placier, P., Cockrell, K. S., Burgoyne, S., Welch, S., Neville, H., & Eferakorho, E. (2006). Theater of the oppressed as an instructional practice. In C. Kosnik, C. Beck, A. R. Freese, & A. P. Samaras (Eds.), *Making a difference in teacher education through self-study: Studies of personal, professional, and program renewal* (pp. 131–146). Dordrecht: Springer.

Richards, J. C. (1998). Turning to the artistic: Developing an enlightened eye by creating teaching self-portraits. In M. L. Hamilton, with S. Pinnegar, T. Russell, J. Loughran, & V. LaBoskey (Eds.), *Reconceptualizing teacher practice: Self-study in teacher education* (pp. 34–44). London: Falmer Press.

Samaras, A. P., with Reed, R. L. (2000). Transcending traditional boundaries through drama: Interdisciplinary teaching and perspective-taking. In J. Loughran & T. Russell (Eds.), *Exploring myths and legends of teacher education.* Proceedings of the Third International Conference on Self-Study of Teacher Education Practices, Herstmonceux Castle East Sussex, England (pp. 218–222). Kingston, ON: Queen's University.

Samaras, A. P., Straits, S. A., & Patrick, S. S. (1998). Collaborating through movement across disciplines and schools. *Teaching Education, 9*(2), 11–20.

Weber, S., & Mitchell, C. (1996). Using drawings to interrogate professional identity and the popular culture of teaching. In I. Goodson & A. Hargreaves (Eds.), *Teachers' professional lives.* London: Falmer Press. (pp. 109–126).

Weber, S., & Mitchell, C. (2000). Prom dresses are us? Excerpts from collective memory work. In J. Loughran & T. Russell (Eds.), *Exploring myths and legends of teacher education.* Proceedings of the Third International Conference on Self-study of Teacher Education Practices, Herstmonceux Castle, East Sussex, England (pp. 248–251). Kingston, ON: Queen's University.

Weber, S., & Mitchell, C. (2002). Academic literary performance, embodiment, and self-study: When the shoe doesn't fit: Death of a salesman. In C. Kosnik, A. Freese, & A. P. Samaras (Eds.), *Making a difference in teacher education through self-study.* Proceedings of the Fourth International Conference on Self-study of Teacher

Education Practices, Herstmonceux Castle, East Sussex, England (Vol. 2, pp. 122–124). Toronto, ON: OISE, University of Toronto.

Weber, S. J., & Mitchell, C. (1996). Drawing ourselves into teaching: Studying the images that shape and distort teacher education. *Teaching and Teacher Education: An International Journal of Research and Studies, 12*(3), 303–313.

Weber, S. J., & Mitchell, C. (1998). Seeing (through) the teacher's body in self-study. In A. L. Cole & S. Finley (Eds.), *Conversations in community.* Proceedings of the Second International Conference on Self-study of Teacher Education Practices, Herstmonceux Castle, East Sussex, England (pp. 209–212). Kingston, ON: Queen's University.

Classroom Teachers

Austin, T., & Senese, J. C. (2004). Self-study in school teaching: Teachers' perspectives. In J. Loughran, M. L. Hamilton, V. K. LaBoskey, & T. Russell (Eds.), *International handbook of self-study of teaching and teacher education practices* (Vol. 2, pp. 1231–1258). Dordrecht: Kluwer Academic Publishers.

Childs, K. (2005). Just where do I think I'm going?: Working with marginalized and disaffected youths and their self-study. In C. Mitchell, S. Weber, & K. O'Reilly-Scanlon (Eds.), *Just who do we think we are?: Methodologies for autobiography and self-study in teaching.* London: RoutledgeFalmer.

Freese, A., Soong, J., Yoshida, J., & Crookes, G. (1999, April). *Learning about inquiry—Inquiring about learning: Two teachers and two professors engage in collaborative research.* Paper presented at the Annual Meeting of the American Educational Research Association Conference, Montreal.

Freese, A., & Strong, A. (2001, April). *Implementing philosophy for children in a social studies classroom: Self-study of a high school classroom.* Paper presented at the Annual Meeting of the American Educational Research Association Conference, Seattle.

Loughran, J. J., Mitchell, I. J., & Mitchell, J. (Eds.). (2002). *Learning from teacher research* (pp. 142–153). New York: Teachers College Press.

Loughran, J. J. (2003). Exploring the nature of teacher research. In Anthony Clarke & Gaalen Erickson (Eds.), *Teacher Research.* London: Routledge/Falmer.

Pereira, P. (2005). Becoming a teacher of mathematics. *Studying Teacher Education: A Journal of Self-Study of Teacher Education Practices, 1*(1), 69–83.

Russell, T. (2006). How 20 years of self-study changed my teaching. In C. Kosnik, C. Beck, A. R. Freese, & A. P. Samaras (Eds.), *Making a difference in teacher education through self-study: Studies of personal, professional, and program renewal* (pp. 3–17). Dordrecht: Springer.

Samaras, A. P., Beck, A., Freese, A. R., & Kosnik, C. (2005). Self-study supports new teachers' professional development. *Focus on Teacher Education Quarterly, 6*(1), 3–5, 7.

Samaras, A. P., & Freese, A. F. (2006). *Self-study of teaching practices primer.* New York: Peter Lang.

Senese, J. (2002). Opposites attract: What I learned about being a classroom teacher by being a teacher educator. In J. J. Loughran & T. Russell (Eds.), *Improving teacher education practices through self-study* (pp. 43–55). London: Routledge/Falmer.

Senese, J. (2005). Teach to learn. *Studying teacher education: A Journal of Self-Study of Teacher Education Practices, 1*(1), 43–54.

Wilcox, S., Watson, J., & Paterson, M. (2004). Self-study in professional practice. In J. J. Loughran, M. L. Hamilton, V. K. LaBoskey, & T. Russell (Eds.), *International handbook of self-study of teaching and teacher education practices* (Vol. 1, pp. 273–312). Dordrecht: Kluwer Academic Publishers.

Educational Reform/Leadership

Arizona Group: Pinnegar, S., Guilfoyle, K., Hamilton, M. L., Placier, P. (1995). Becoming teachers of teachers: Alternative paths expressed in beginners' voices. In F. Korthagen & T. Russell (Eds.), *Teachers who teach teachers: Reflections on teacher education* (pp. 35–55). London: Falmer Press.

Arizona Group: Guilfoyle, K., Hamilton, M. L., Pinnegar, S. & Pacier, P. (1996). Negotiating balance between reforming teacher education and forming self as teacher educator, *Teacher Education Quarterly, 23*(3), 153–168.

Arizona Group: Guilfoyle, K., Hamilton, M. L., & Pinnegar, S. (1997). Obligations to unseen children. In J. J. Loughran & T. Russell (Eds.), *Teaching about teaching: Purpose, passion, and pedagogy in teacher education* (pp. 183–209). London: Falmer Press.

Arizona Group: Guilfoyle, K., Hamilton, M. L., Pinnegar, S. & Placier, P. (1999). Negotiating balance between reforming teacher education and forming self as teacher educator. In A. L. Cole, R. Elijah, & J. G. Knowles, (Eds.), *The heart of the matter: Teacher educators and teacher education reform* (pp. 171–192). San Francisco: Caddo Gap Press.

Bodone, F., Guðjónsdóttir, H., & Dalmau, M. (2004). Revisioning and recreating practice: Collaboration in self-study. In J. J. Loughran, M. L. Hamilton, V. K. LaBoskey, & T. Russell (Eds.), *International handbook of self-study of teaching and teacher education practices* (Vol. 1, pp. 743–784). Dordrecht: Kluwer Academic Publishers.

Cole, A. L., Elijah, R., & Knowles, J. G. (Eds.). (1998). *The heart of the matter: Teacher educators and teacher education reform*. San Francisco: Caddo Gap Press.

Cole, A. L., & Knowles, J. G. (2004). Research, practice, and academia in North America. In J. J. Loughran, M. L. Hamilton, V. K. LaBoskey, & T. Russell (Eds.), *International handbook of self-study of teaching and teacher education practices* (Vol. 1, pp. 451–482). Dordrecht: Kluwer Academic Publishers.

Freese, A. (1995, April). *Bridging the theory-practice gap through self-study*. Paper presented at the Annual Meeting of the American Educational Research Association Conference, San Francisco.

Freese, A. (1997, March). *The role of reflection on preservice teacher development in the context of a professional development school*. Paper presented at the Annual Meeting of the American Educational Research Association Conference, Chicago.

Freese, A. R. (1998). A learning community reshapes a teacher preparation program through self-study and reflection. In A. L. Cole & S. Finley (Eds.), *Conversations in Community*. Proceedings of the Second International Conference on Self Study in Teacher Education Practices, Herstmonceux, East Sussex, England (pp. 88–91). Kingston, ON: Queen's University.

Hoban, G. F. (Ed.). (2005). *The missing links in teacher education design*. Dordrecht: Kluwer Academic Publishers.

Hopper, T., & Sanford, K. (2004). Self-Study from participating in school integrated teacher education communities of practice. In D. Tidwell, L. Fitzgerald, & M. Heston (Eds.), *Risking the journey of self-study in a diverse world*. Proceedings of the Fifth International Conference on

Self-Study of Teacher Education Practices, Herstmonceux Castle, East Sussex, England (pp. 149–152). Cedar Falls, IA: University of Northern Iowa.

Korthagen, F., & Lunenberg, M. (2004). Links between self-study and teacher education reform. In J. J. Loughran, M. L. Hamilton, V. K. LaBoskey & T. Russell (Eds.), *International handbook of self-study of teaching and teacher education practices* (Vol. 1, pp. 421–449). Dordrecht: Kluwer Academic Publishers.

Kosnik, C., Beck, C., Freese, A. R., & Samaras, A. P. (Eds.), (2006). *Making a difference in teacher education through self-study: Studies of personal, professional, and program renewal*. Dordrecht: Springer.

Kosnik, C., Freese, A. R., & Samaras, A. P. (2002). Searching for integrity of our research to our practices in three teacher education programs. In C. Kosnik, A. Freese, & A. P. Samaras (Eds.), (2002). *Making a difference in teacher education through self-study*. Proceedings of the Fourth International Conference on Self-Study of Teacher Education Practices, Herstmonceux Castle, East Sussex, England (Vol. 2, pp. 48–53). Toronto, ON: OISE, University of Toronto.

Manke, M. P. (2004). Administrators also do self-study: Issues of power and community, social justice, and teacher education reform. In J. J. Loughran, M. L. Hamilton, V. K. LaBoskey, & T. Russell (Eds.), *International handbook of self-study of teaching and teacher education practices* (Vol. 2, pp. 1367–1391). Dordrecht: Kluwer Academic Publishers.

Samaras, A. P. (1998). Finding my way: Teaching methods courses from a sociocultural perspective. In A. L. Cole, R. Elijah, & J. G. Knowles (Eds.), *The heart of the matter: Teacher educators and teacher education reform* (pp. 55–79). San Francisco: Caddo Gap Press.

Samaras, A. P. (2002). *Self-study for teacher educators: Crafting a pedagogy for educational change*. New York: Peter Lang.

Intersections Among Self-Study/Teacher/Learner

Clift, R. T., Brady, P., Mora, R. A., Choi, S. J., & Stegemoller, J. (2006). From self-study to collaborative self-study to collaborative self-study of collaboration: Evolution of a research team. In C. Kosnik, C. Beck, A. R. Freese, & A. P. Samaras (Eds.), *Making a difference in teacher education through self-study: Studies of personal, professional, and program renewal* (pp. 85–100). Dordrecht: Springer.

Macintyre Latta, M., & Olafson, L. (2006). Identities in the making: Realized in-between self and other. *Studying Teacher Education 2(1), 77-90.*

Sandholtz, J. H. (2005). Analyzing teaching through student work. *Teacher Education Quarterly, 32*(3), 107–122.

Methodology of Self-Study

Barnes, D. (1998). Forward: Looking forward: The concluding remarks at the Castle Conference. In M. L. Hamilton, with S. Pinnegar, T. Russell, J. Loughran, & V. LaBoskey (Eds.), *Reconceptualizing teaching practice: Self-study in teacher education* (pp. ix-xiv). London: Falmer Press.

Bullough, R. V., Jr,. & Gitlin, A. (1995). *Becoming a student of teaching: Methodologies for exploring self and school context.* New York: Garland Publishers.

Bullough, R.V., Jr., & Pinnegar, S. E. (2001). Guidelines for quality in autobiographical forms of self-study research. *Educational Researcher, 30*(3), 13–22.

Coia, L., & Taylor, M. (2006). From the inside out, and the outside in: Co/autoethnography as a means of professional renewal. In C. Kosnik, C. Beck, A. R. Freese, & A. P. Samaras (Eds.), *Making a difference in teacher education through self-study: Studies of personal, professional, and program renewal* (pp.19–33). Dordrecht: Springer.

Feldman, A. (2003). Validity and quality in self-study. *Educational Researcher, 32*(3), 26–28.

Feldman, A. (2006). Using an existential form of reflection to understand my transformation as a teacher educator. In C. Kosnik, C. Beck, A. R. Freese, & A. P. Samaras (Eds.), *Making a difference in teacher education through self-study: Studies of personal, professional, and program renewal* (pp. 35–49). Dordrecht: Springer.

Feldman, A., Paugh, P., & Mills, G. (2004). Self-study through action research. In J. Loughran, M. L. Hamilton, V. K. LaBoskey, & J. Russell (Eds.), *International handbook of self-study of teaching and teacher education practices* (Vol. 2, pp. 943–977). Dordrecht: Springer.

Gudðjónsdóttir, H. (2004). Self-study and pragmatism. In D. Tidwell, L. Fitzgerald, & M. Heston (Eds.), *Risking the journey of self-study in a diverse world.* Proceedings of the Fifth International Conference on Self-Study of Teacher Education Practices, Herstmonceux Castle, East Sussex, England (pp. 141–144). Cedar Falls, IA: University of Northern Iowa.

Guilfoyle, K., Hamilton, M. L., & Pinnegar, S. (2004). The epistemological dimensions and dynamics of professional dialogue in self-study. In J. J. Loughran, M. L. Hamilton, V. K. LaBoskey, & T. Russell (Eds.), *International handbook of self-study of teaching and teacher education practices* (Vol. 2, pp. 1109–1167). Dordrecht: Kluwer Academic Publishers.

Ham, V., & Kane, R. (2004). Finding a way through the swamp: A case for self-study as research. In J. J. Loughran, M. L. Hamilton, V. K. LaBoskey, & T. Russell (Eds.), *International handbook of self-study of teaching and teacher education practices* (Vol. 1, pp. 103–150). Dordrecht: Kluwer Academic Publishers.

Hamilton, M. L., & Pinnegar, S. (2000). On the threshold of a new century: Trustworthiness, integrity, and self-study in teacher education. *Journal of Teacher Education, 51*(3), 234–240.

LaBoskey, V. K. (2004). The methodology of self-study and its theoretical underpinnings. In J. J. Loughran, M. L. Hamilton, V. K. LaBoskey, & T. Russell (Eds.), *International handbook of self-study of teaching and teacher education practices* (Vol. 2., pp. 817–869). Dordrecht: Kluwer Academic Publishers.

LaBoskey, V. K. (2004). Afterword: Moving the methods of self-study research and practice forward: Challenges and opportunities. In J. J. Loughran, M. L. Hamilton, V. K. LaBoskey, & T. Russell (Eds.), *International handbook of self-study of teaching and teacher education practices* (Vol. 2, pp. 1169–1184). Dordrecht: Kluwer Academic Publishers.

Lighthall, F. F. (2004). Fundamental features and approaches of the s-step enterprise. In J. J. Loughran, M. L. Hamilton, V. K. LaBoskey, & T. Russell (Eds.), *International handbook of self-study of teaching and teacher education practices* (Vol. 1, pp. 193–245). Dordrecht: Kluwer Academic Publishers.

Loughran, J., & Northfield, J. (1998). A framework for the development of self-study practice. In M. L. Hamilton, with S. Pinnegar, T. Russell, J. Loughran, & V. K. LaBoskey (Eds.), *Reconceptualizing teaching practice: Self-study in teacher education* (pp. 7–18). London: Falmer Press.

Lyons, N., & Freidus, (2004). The reflective portfolio in self-study: Inquiring into and representing knowledge about practice. In J. J. Loughran, M. L. Hamilton, V. K. LaBoskey, & T. Russell (Eds.), *International handbook of self-study of teaching and teacher education practices* (Vol. 2, pp. 1073–1107). Dordrecht: Kluwer Academic Publishers.

Mitchell, C., Weber, S., & O'Reilly-Scanlon, K. (2005). *Just who do we think we are? Methodologies for autobiography and self-study.* London: RoutledgeFalmer.

Pinnegar, S. (1998). Introduction to Methodology. In M. L. Hamilton, with S. Pinnegar, T. Russell, J. Loughran, & V. K. LaBoskey (Eds.), *Reconceptualizing the education of teachers: Self-study in teacher education* (pp. 31–33). London: Falmer.

Pinnegar, S., & Hamilton, M. L. (1998). Introduction. In M. L. Hamilton, with S. Pinnegar, T. Russell, J. Loughran, & V. K. LaBoskey (Eds.), *Reconceptualizing the education of teachers: Self-study in teacher education* (pp. 1–4). London: Falmer.

Pinnegar, S., & Hamilton, M. L. (1998). Conclusion. In M. L. Hamilton, with S. Pinnegar, T. Russell, J. J. Loughran, & V. K. LaBoskey (Eds.), *Reconceptualizing the education of teachers: Self-study in teacher education.* (pp. 235–246). London: Falmer.

Russell, T., & Schuck, S. (2004). How critical are critical friends and how critical should they be? In D. Tidwell, L. Fitzgerald & M. Heston (Eds.), *Risking the journey of self-study in a diverse world.* Proceedings of the Fifth International Conference on Self-Study of Teacher Education Practices, Herstmonceux Castle, East Sussex, England (pp. 213–216). Cedar Falls, IA: University of Northern Iowa.

Samaras, A. P., Hicks, M. A., & Berger, J. G. (2004). Self-study through personal history. In J. J. Loughran, M. L. Hamilton, V. K. LaBoskey, & T. Russell (Eds.), *International handbook of self-study of teaching and teacher education practices* (Vol. 2, pp. 905–942). Dordrecht: Kluwer Academic Publishers.

Weber, S., & Mitchell, C. (2004). Visual artistic modes of representation for self-study. In J. J. Loughran, M. L. Hamilton, V. K. LaBoskey, & T. Russell (Eds.), *International handbook of self-study of teaching and teacher education practices* (Vol. 2, pp. 979–1038). Dordrecht: Kluwer Academic Publishers.

Whitehead, J. (2004). What counts as evidence in self-studies of teacher education practices? In J. J. Loughran, M. L. Hamilton, V. K. LaBoskey, & T. Russell (Eds.), *International handbook of self-study of teaching and teacher education practices* (Vol. 2, pp. 871–903). Dordrecht:

Kluwer Academic Publishers.

Preservice Teachers

Aubusson, P., & Schuck, S. (2006). *Teacher learning and development: The mirror maze.* Dordrecht: Kluwer/Springer.

Beck, C., Freese, A. R., & Kosnik, C. (2004). The preservice practicum: Learning through self-study in a professional setting. In J. J. Loughran, M. L. Hamilton, V. K. LaBoskey, & T. Russell (Eds.), *International handbook of self-study of teaching and teacher education practices* (Vol. 2, pp. 1259–1293). Dordrecht: Kluwer Academic Publishers.

Berry, A. (2004a). Confidence and uncertainty in teaching about teaching. *Australian Journal of Education, 48*(2), 149–166.

Berry, A. (2004b). Learning about helping student teachers learn about their practice: Revisited. In D. Tidwell, L. Fitzgerald & M. Heston (Eds.), *Journeys of hope: Risking self-study in a diverse world.* The Fifth International Conference on self-study of teacher education practices, Herstmonceux Castle, East Sussex, England (pp. 37–40). Cedar Falls, IA: University of Northern Iowa.

Berry, A. (2004c). Self-study in teaching about teaching. In Loughran, J. J., Hamilton, M. L., LaBoskey, V. & Russell, T. (Eds.), *International handbook of self-study of teaching and teacher education practices* (Vol. 2, pp. 1295–1332). Dordrecht: Kluwer Academic Publishers.

Berry, A., & Loughran, J. J. (2000). Developing an understanding of learning to teach in teacher education. In J. J. Loughran & T. L. Russell (Eds.), *Exploring myths and legends of teacher education.* Proceedings of the Third International Conference on Self-Study of Teacher Education Practices, Herstmonceux Castle, East Sussex, England (pp. 25–29). Kingston, ON: Queen's University.

Berry, A., & Loughran, J. J. (2002). Developing an understanding of learning to teach in teacher education. In J. J. Loughran & T. Russell (Eds.), *Improving teacher education practices through self-study* (pp. 13–29). London: Routledge.

Berry, A., & Loughran, J. J. (2005). Teaching about teaching: The role of self-study. In S. Weber, C. Mitchell & K. O'Reilly-Scanlon (Eds.), *Just who do we think we are? Methodologies for self-study in teacher education* (pp. 168–180). London: Routledge/Falmer.

Freese, A. R. (1999). The role of reflection on preservice

teachers' development in the context of a professional development school. *Teaching and Teacher Education, 15*(8), 895–910.

Freese, A. R. (2006). Transformation through self-study: The voices of preservice teachers. In C. Kosnik, C. Beck, A. R. Freese, & A. P. Samaras (Eds.), *Making a difference in teacher education through self-study: Studies of personal, professional, and program renewal* (pp. 65–83). Dordrecht: Springer.

Freese, A. R. (2006). Reframing one's teaching: Discovering our teacher selves through reflection and inquiry. *Teaching and Teacher Education, 22* (1) 100–119.

Hamilton, M. L., LaBoskey, V., Loughran, J. J., Russell, T. L. (1998). Have five years of self-study changed teacher education? Artifacts of our personal development as teacher educators. In A. L. Cole & S. Finley (Eds.), *Conversations in community.* Proceedings of the Second International Conference on Self Study in Teacher Education Practices, Herstmonceux, East Sussex, England (pp. 1–5). Queen's University: Kingston, Ontario, Canada.

Hamilton, M. L., with Pinnegar, S., Russell, T., Loughran, J., LaBoskey, V. (Eds.). (1998). *Reconceptualizing teaching practice: Self-study in teacher education.* London: Falmer Press.

Holt, D. H. (2004). Personal history-based beliefs as relevant prior knowledge in course work. In J. J. Loughran, M. L. Hamilton, V. K. LaBoskey, & T. Russell (Eds.), *The international handbook of self-study of teaching and teacher education practices* (Vol. 1, pp. 345–367). Dordrecht: Kluwer Academic Publishers.

Hopper, T. F. (2000). Personal construct psychology for developing reflective teaching in physical education: A story of decentering 'self' as teacher. *AVANTE* Journal, *6(3)*,1–11.

Loughran, J. J. (1996). *Developing reflective practitioners: Learning about teaching and learning through modeling.* London: Falmer Press.

Loughran, J. J. (1997). Learning through modeling: Developing pre-service teachers' understanding of reflection. *Teaching Education, 8*(2), 23–28.

Loughran, J. J. (1997). Teaching about teaching: Principles and practice. In J. J. Loughran & T. Russell (Eds.), *Teaching about teaching: Purpose, passion and pedagogy in teacher education* (pp. 57–70). London: Falmer Press.

Loughran, J. J. (2002). Understanding self-study of teacher education practices. In J. J. Loughran & T. Russell (Eds.), *Improving teacher education practices through self-study* (pp. 239–248). London: Routledge.

Loughran, J. J. (2003). Pursuing scholarship in teacher education. In D. Fraser & R. Openshaw (Eds.), *Informing our practice.* Special Volume. Selections from the Teacher Education Forum of Aotearoa New Zealand 2002 (pp. 141–155). Palmerston North, N.Z.: Kanuka Grove Press.

Loughran, J. J. (2003). In search of meaning in teaching about teaching: Self-study of teacher education practices. *International Journal of Educational Policy, Research and Practice, 4*(2), 3–38.

Loughran, J. J. (2004). Practitioner research in teacher education: Self-study of teacher education practices. *Didaktisk Tidskrift: För practiker och forskare (Nordic Journal of Teaching and Learning: For practitioners and researchers), 14* (1), 5–15.

Loughran, J. J. (2004). Understanding teaching about teaching: Teacher educators' researching their own practice. *VELON, 25*(3), 23–28.

Loughran, J. J. (2004). Informing practice: Developing knowledge of teaching about teaching. In D. Tidwell, L. Fitzgerald, & M. Heston (Eds.), *Journeys of hope: Risking self-study in a diverse world.* Proceedings of the Fifth International Conference on Self-Study of Teacher Education Practices, Herstmonceux Castle, East Sussex, England (pp. 186–189). Cedar Falls, IA: University of Northern Iowa.

Loughran, J. J. (2004). A history and context of self-study of teaching and teacher education practices. In J. J. Loughran, M. L. Hamilton, V. K. LaBoskey, & T. L. Russell (Eds.), *International handbook of self-study of teaching and teacher education practices* (Vol. 1, pp. 7–39). Dordrecht: Kluwer Academic Publishers.

Loughran, J. J. (2004). Learning through self-study. In J. J. Loughran, M. L. Hamilton, V. K. LaBoskey, & T. Russell (Eds.), *International handbook of self-study of teaching and teacher education practices* (Vol. 1, pp. 151–192). Dordrecht: Kluwer Academic Publishers.

Loughran, J. J. (2005). Researching teaching about teaching: Self-study of teacher education practices. *Studying Teacher Education: A Journal of Self-Study of Teacher Education Practices, 1*(1), 5–16.

Loughran, J. J. (2006). *Developing a pedagogy of teacher edu-*

cation: Understanding teaching and learning about teaching. London: Routledge.

Loughran, J. J. (2006). Challenges, dilemmas and future directions in teaching about teaching. In P. Aubusson & S. Schuck (Eds.), *Teaching, learning and development: The mirror maze.* Dordrecht: Kluwer/Springer.

Loughran, J. J. , & Berry, A. (2005). Modeling by teacher educators. *Teaching and Teacher Education, 21*(2), 193–203.

Loughran, J. J., Berry, A., & Corrigan, D. (2001). Once were science teachers. *The Qualitative Report, 6*(4) (December). http://www.nova.edu/ssss/QR/QR6–4/loughran.html

Loughran, J. J., Berry, A., & Tudball, L. (2002). Teaching about teaching: Learning to help student-teachers learn about their practice. In C. Kosnik, A. R. Freese, & A. P. Samaras (Eds.), *Making a difference in teacher education through self-study.* Proceedings of the Fourth International Conference on Self-Study of Teacher Education Practices, Herstmonceux Castle, East Sussex, England (pp. 67–71). Toronto, ON: OISE, Toronto University.

Loughran, J. J., Berry, A., & Tudball, L. (2006). Collaborative learning in teaching about teaching. In C. Kosnik, A. R. Freese, & A. P. Samaras (Eds.), *Making a difference in teacher education through self-study: Studies of personal, professional, and program renewal* (pp. 203–225). Dordrecht: Springer.

Loughran, J. J., Berry, A., & Tudball, L. (2005). Developing trust in teaching: Learning to help student-teachers learn about their practice. In G. Hoban (Ed.), *The missing links in teacher education* (pp. 193–208). Dordrecht: Kluwer Academic Publishers.

Loughran, J. J., Hamilton, M. L., LaBoskey, V. K., & Russell, T. (Eds.). (2004). *International handbook of self-study of teaching and teacher education practices* (Vols. 1 & 2). Dordrecht: Kluwer Academic Publishers.

Loughran, J. J., & Northfield, J.R. (1996). *Opening the classroom door: Teacher, researcher, learner.* London: Falmer Press.

Loughran, J. J., & Northfield, J. R. (1998). The nature of knowledge development in self-study practice. In M. L. Hamilton, with S. Pinnegar, T. Russell, J. Loughran,. & V. K. LaBoskey (Eds.), *Reconceptualizing teaching practice: Self-study in teacher education* (pp. 7–18). London: Falmer Press.

Loughran, J. J., & Russell, T. (Eds.). (1997). *Teaching about teaching: Purpose, passion and pedagogy in teacher educa-*

tion. London: Falmer Press.

Loughran, J. J., & Russell, T. (Eds.). (2002). *Improving teacher education practices through self-study.* London: Routledge/Falmer.

Northfield, J. R., & Loughran, J. J. (1996). Learning through self-study: Exploring the development of knowledge. In J. Richards & T. Russell (Eds.), *Empowering our future in teacher education.* Proceedings of the First International Conference on Self-study of Teacher Education Practices, Herstmonceux Castle, East Sussex, England (pp. 180–182). Kingston, ON: Queen's University.

Schuck, S. (2002). Using self-study to challenge my teaching practice in mathematics education. *Reflective Practice* 3(3), 327–337.

Schulte, A. K. (2001). Student teachers in transformation: A self-study of a supervisor's practice (Doctoral dissertation, University of Wisconsin, 2001). *Dissertation Abstracts International,* Vol. 62, No. 4, p. 1381 (University Microfilms No. 3012553).

Schulte, A. K. (2005). Assuming my transformation: Transforming my assumptions, *Studying Teacher Education,* 1(1), 31–42.

Volkmann, M. J., Abell, S. K., & Zgagacz, M. (2004). *The challenges of teaching physics to preservice elementary teachers: Orientations of the professor, teaching assistant, and students.* Published online 18 July 2005 in Wiley InterScience (www.interscience.wiley.com).

Processes of Self-Study

Schuck, S., & Russell, T. (2005). Self-Study, critical friendship, and the complexities of teacher education. *Studying Teacher Education,* 1(2), 107–121.

Tidwell, D., & Fitzgerald, L. (2004). Self-study as teaching. In J. J. Loughran, M. L. Hamilton, V. LaBoskey, & T. Russell (Eds.), *International handbook of self-study of teaching and teacher education practices* (Vol. 1, pp. 69–102). Dordrecht: Kluwer Academic Publishers.

Wilkes, G. (1998). Seams of paradoxes in teaching. In M. L. Hamilton, with S. Pinnegar, T. Russell, J. Loughran, & V. K. LaBoskey (Eds.), *Reconceptualizing teaching practice: Self-study in teacher education* (pp. 198–207). London: Falmer Press.

Professional Development

Arizona Group: Pinnegar, S., Guilfoyle, K., Hamilton, M.L., & Placier, P. (1994). Letters from beginners: Negotiating the transition from graduate student to assistant professor. *The Journal, 8*(2),71–82.

Arizona Group: Placier, P., Pinnegar, S., Hamilton, M.L. & Guilfoyle, K. (2006). Exploring the concept of dialogue in the self-study of teaching practices. In C. Kosnik, C. Beck, A. R. Freese, & A. P. Samaras (Eds.), *Making a difference in teacher education through self-study* (pp. 51–64) Dordrecht: Springer.

Chan, F. N. K. (2004). Crossing the border: Identity and education: Anarrative self-study. Unpublished doctoral dissertation, OISE/University of Toronto, Toronto. *Dissertation Abstracts International,* (University Microfilms No. AAT NQ94280).

Freese, A. R. (2004). Innovation and change in teacher education: An inquiring, reflective, collaborative approach. In G. Hoban (Ed.), *The missing links in teacher education: Innovative approaches for designing teacher education programs* (pp. 83–101). Dordrecht: Kluwer Academic Publishers.

Freese, A. (2004). Using the voices of students as a text for my teaching. In D. Tidwell, L. Fitzgerald, & M. Heston (Eds.), *Risking the journey of self-study in a diverse world.* Proceedings of the Fifth International Conference on Self-Study of Teacher Education Practices, Herstmonceux Castle, East Sussex, England (pp. 113–116). Cedar Falls, Iowa: University of Northern Iowa.

Freese, A., Kosnik, C., & LaBoskey, V. (2000). Three teacher educators explore their understandings and practices of self-study and reflection. In J. Loughran & T. Russell (Eds.), *Exploring myths and legends of teacher education.* Proceedings of the Third International Conference on Self-Study of Teacher Education Practices, Herstmonceux Castle, East Sussex, England (pp. 116–120). Kingston, Ontario: Queen's University.

Gipe, J. P. (1998). Self-study on teacher education practices through the use of faculty course portfolio. In M. L. Hamilton, with S. Pinnegar, T. Russell, J. J. Loughran, & V. K. LaBoskey (Eds.), *Reconceptualizing teaching practice: Self-study in teacher education* (pp. 140–146). London: Falmer Press.

Griffiths, M. (1998). Telling stories about collaboration:

Secrets and lies? In A. L. Cole & S. Finley (Eds.), *Conversations in community.* Proceedings of the Second International Conference on Self-study of Teacher Education Practices, Herstmonceux Castle, East Sussex, England (pp. 225–228). Kingston, ON: Queen's University.

Griffiths, M., & Poursanidou, D. (2005). A self-study of collaborations among teacher educators, *Studying Teacher Education, 1*(2), 141–158.

Kitchen, J. (2005). Conveying respect and empathy: Becoming a relational teacher educator. *Studying Teacher Education, 1*(2), 194–207.

Kitchen, J. (2005). Looking backwards, moving forward: Understanding my narrative as a teacher educator. *Studying Teacher Education, 1*(1), 17–30.

Kosnik, C., Freese, A. R., & Samaras, A. P. (2002). Searching for integrity of our research to our practices in three teacher education programs. In C. Kosnik, A. Freese, & A. P. Samaras (Eds.), *Making a difference in teacher education through self-study.* Proceedings of the Fourth International Conference on the Self-Study of Teacher Education Practices, Herstmonceux Castle, East Sussex, England (Vol. 1, pp. 48–53). Toronto, ON: OISE, University of Toronto.

Macintyre Latta, M. (2005). The role and place of fear in what it means to teach and to learn. *Teaching Education, 16*(3), 183–196.

Muchmore, J. A. (2004). *A teacher's life: Stories of literacy, teacher thinking, and professional development.* San Francisco: Caddo Gap Press, & Halifax, NS: Backalong Books.

Oda, L. K. (1998). Harmony, conflict and respect: An Asian-American educator's self-study. In M. L. Hamilton, with S. Pinnegar, T. Russell, J. Loughran, & V. K. LaBoskey (Eds.), *Reconceptualizing teaching practice: Self-study in teacher education* (pp. 113–123). London: Falmer Press.

Pinnegar, S. (1995). (Re)Experiencing Beginning. *Teacher Education Quarterly, 22*(3), 65–84.

Pinnegar, S. (1995). (Re) Experiencing Student Teaching. In F. Korthagen & T. Russell (Eds.), *Teachers who teach teachers: Reflections on teacher education* (pp. 56–70). London: Falmer Press.

Pinnegar, S. (1996). Sharing Stories: A teacher educator accounting for narrative in her teaching. *Action in Teacher Education, 18*(3), 13–22.

Pinnegar, S. (1996). Depending on experience. *Educational Research Quarterly, 2*(2), 43–59.

Pinnegar, S. (2005). Identity development, moral authority and the teacher educator. In G. Hoban (Ed.), *The Missing links in teacher education design: Developing a conceptual framework* (pp. 259–279). Dordrecht: Springer.

Pinnegar, S., Lay, C., Bigham, S., & Dulude, C. (2005). Teaching as highlighted by mothering: A narrative inquiry. *Studying Teacher Education, 1*(1), 55–67.

Russell, T., & Pinnegar, S. (1995). Introduction for special guest edition on self-study in teacher education. *Teacher Education Quarterly, 22*(3), 5–10.

Samaras, A. P. (1995). My journey to Ithaca: Reflections of a teacher educator. *Teaching Education, 7*(1), 96–101.

Samaras, A. P., DeMulder, E. K., Kayler, M.A., Newton, L., Rigsby, L. C., Weller, K.L., & Wilcox, D. R. (2006). Spheres of learning in teacher collaboration. In C. Kosnik, C. Beck, A. R. Freese, & A. P., Samaras, (Eds.), *Making a difference in teacher education through self-study: Studies of personal, professional, and program renewal* (pp. 147–163). Dordrecht: Kluwer Academic Publishers.

Samaras, A. P., Hicks, M. A., Garvey Berger, J. (2004). Self-study through personal history. In J. J. Loughran, M. L. Hamilton, V. K. LaBoskey, & T. Russell (Eds.), *International handbook of self-study of teaching and teacher education practices* (Vol. 2, pp. 905–942). Dordrecht: Kluwer Academic Publishers.

Samaras, A. P., Kayler, M.A., Rigsby, L.C., Weller, K. L., & Wilcox, D. R. (2006). Self-study of the craft of faculty team teaching in a non-traditional teacher education program. *Studying Teacher Education, 2*(1), 43–57.

Social Justice/Diversity

Brown, E. R. (2002). The (in)visibility of race in narrative constructions of the self. In J. J. Loughran & T. Russell (Eds.), *Improving teacher education practices through self-study* (pp. 145–160). London: Falmer Press.

Brown, E. R. (2004). The significance of race and social class for self-study and the professional knowledge based of teacher education. In J. J. Loughran, M. L. Hamilton, V. LaBoskey, & T. Russell (Eds.), *International handbook of self-study of teaching and teacher education practices* (Vol. 1, pp. 517–574). Dordrecht: Kluwer Academic Publishers.

Freese, A., Strong, A. (2006, April). *Multicultural education and self-study: A personal, collaborative, constructivist approach.* Paper presented at the Annual Meeting of the American Educational Research Association Conference, San Francisco.

Griffiths, M. (1996). Know thyself: Philosophy/self-study empowering our future in teacher education through self-study. In J. Richards & T. Russell (Eds.), *Empowering our future in teacher education.* Proceedings of the First International Conference on Self-study of Teacher Education Practices, Herstmonceux Castle, East Sussex, England (pp. 87–91). Kingston, ON: Queen's University.

Griffiths, M. (2002). 'Nothing grand': Small tales and working for social justice. In J. J. Loughran & T. Russell (Eds.), *Improving teacher education practices through self-study* (pp. 161–175). London: Routledge/Falmer.

Griffiths, M., Bass, L., Johnston, M., & Perselli, V. (2004). Knowledge, social justice, and self-study. In J. J. Loughran, M. L. Hamilton, V. LaBoskey, & T. Russell (Eds.), *International handbook of self-study of teaching and teacher education practices* (Vol. 1, pp. 651–707). Dordrecht: Kluwer Academic Publishers.

Griffiths, M., & Windle, J. (2002). Helping teacher educators learn to research: Bread and roses—And a phoenix. In C. Kosnik, A. Freese, & A. P. Samaras (Eds.), *Making a difference in teacher education through self-study.* Proceedings of the Fourth International Conference on Self-study of Teacher Education Practices, Herstmonceux Castle, East Sussex, England (Vol. 1, pp. 87—91). Toronto, ON: OISE, University of Toronto.

Griffiths, M., Windle, J., & Simms, M. (2006). 'That's what I am here for': Images of working lives of academic and support staff. In D. Tidwell, & L. Fitzgerald (Eds.), *Self-study and diversity* (pp. 227-248). Rotterdam, The Netherlands: Sense Publishers.

Gudðjónsdóttir, H. (2004). How are teachers prepared to teach students with learning disabilities in mathematics? In D. Tidwell, L. Fitzgerald, & M. Heston (Eds.), *Risking the journey of self-study in a diverse world.* Proceedings of the Fifth International Conference on Self-Study of Teacher Education Practices, Herstmonceux Castle, East Sussex, England (pp. 137–140). Cedar Falls, IA: University of Northern Iowa.

Hamilton, M. L. (2002). Change, social justice, and re-liability: Reflections of a secret (change) agent. In J. J.

Loughran & T. Russell (Eds.), *Improving teacher education practices through self-study* (pp. 176–189). London: Routledge/Falmer.

Pereira, P. (2005). Becoming a teacher of mathematics. *Studying teacher education: A journal of self-study of teacher education practices,* 1(1), 31–42.

Schulte, A. K., & Genor, M. (2002). Exploring Race: Teacher educators bridge their personal and professional identities. *Multicultural Perspectives,* 4(3), 15–20.

Schulte, A. K. (2004). Examples of practice: Professional knowledge and self-study in multicultural teacher education. In J. J. Loughran, M. L. Hamilton, V. K. LaBoskey, & T. L. Russell (Eds.), *International handbook of self-study of teaching and teacher education Practices* (Vol. 1, pp. 709–742). Dordrecht: Kluwer Academic Publishers.

Schulte, A. K. (2005). Assuming my transformation: Transforming my assumptions. *Studying Teacher Education,* 1(1), 31–42.

Seaton, L. (2004). Learning to be a gender equity consultant: Listening to teachers. In D. Tidwell, L. Fitzgerald, & M. Heston (Eds.), *Risking the journey of self-study in a diverse world.* Proceedings of the Fifth International Conference on Self-Study of Teacher Education Practices (pp. 217–220). Herstmonceux Castle, East Sussex, England, Cedar Falls, IA: University of Northern Iowa.

SooHoo, S. (2006). *Talking leaves: Narratives of otherness.* Cresskill, NJ: Hampton Press.

Spraggins, T. (2004). A self-study of internalized racism and educational discourse. In D. Tidwell, L. Fitzgerald, & M. Heston (Eds.), *Risking the journey of self-study in a diverse world.* Proceedings of the Fifth International Conference on Self-Study of Teacher Education Practices, Herstmonceux Castle, East Sussex, England (pp. 225–228). Cedar Falls, IA: University of Northern Iowa.

Tidwell, D., & Fitzgerald, L. M. (Eds.). (2006). *Self-study and diversity.* Rotterdam, The Netherlands: Sense Publishers.

Tudball, L. (2004). Listening and responding to the views of my students: Are they ready to teach in a diverse world? Risking self-study of the internationalization of teacher education. In D. Tidwell, L. Fitzgerald, & M. Heston (Eds.), *Risking the journey of self-study in a diverse world.* Proceedings of the Fifth International Conference on Self-Study of Teacher Education Practices, Herstmonceux Castle, East Sussex, England (pp. 250–254).

Cedar Falls, IA: University of Northern Iowa.

Technology

Berry, A. (2004). Making the private public: Giving preservice teachers access to their teacher educators' thinking via an electronic journal. *Didaktisk Tidskrift Nordic Journal of Teaching and Learning, 14*(1), 17–24.

Ham, V., & Davey, R. (2006). Is virtual teaching, real teaching? Learnings from two self-studies. In C. Kosnik, C. Beck, A. R. Freese, & A. P. Samaras (Eds.), *Making a difference in teacher education through self-study: Studies of personal, professional, and program renewal* (pp. 101–116). Dordrecht: Springer.

Hoban, G. F. (1997). Learning to learn in the context of a science methods course. In J. J. Loughran & T. Russell (Eds.), *Teaching about teaching: Purpose, passion and pedagogy in teacher education* (pp. 133–149). London: The Falmer Press.

Hoban, G. F. (2001). Using the web for reflection on how learning occurs in university classes. In J. J. Hedberg (Ed.), *Online learning environments: Research and teaching* (pp. 69–81). Wollongong: University of Wollongong.

Hoban, G. F. (2002). Using technology for self-study practices in teacher education. In C. Kosnik, A. R, Freese, & A. P. Samaras (Eds.), *Making a difference in teacher education through self-study.* Proceedings of the Fourth International Conference on the Self-Study of Teacher Education Practices, Herstmonceux Castle, East Sussex, England (Vol. 2, pp. 9–13).Toronto, ON: OISE, University of Toronto.

Hoban, G. F. (2003). Using the World Wide Web for researching teaching-learning relationships. In A. Clarke & G. Erickson (Eds.), *Teacher inquiry* (pp. 129–140). London and New York: Routledge/Falmer.

Hoban, G. F. (2004). Using information and communication technologies for the self-study of teaching. In J. J. Loughran, M. L. Hamilton, V. K. LaBoskey, & T. Russell (Eds.), *International handbook of self-study of teaching and teacher education practices* (Vol. 2, pp. 1039–1072). Dordrecht: Kluwer Academic Publishers.

Hoban, G. F. (2005). Seeking quality and coherence in a conceptual framework for teacher education design. In G. F. Hoban (Ed.), *The missing links in teacher education design: A multi-linked approach for generating a con-*

ceptual framework (pp. 1–17). Dordrecht: Kluwer Academic Publishers.

Hoban, G. F. (2005). Using a multi-linked approach for generating a conceptual framework. In G. F. Hoban (Ed.), *The missing links in teacher education design: A multi-linked approach for generating a conceptual framework* (pp. 281–291). Dordrecht: Kluwer Academic Publishers.

Hoban, G. F., & Brickell, G. (2006). Using diagrams as reflective tools to represent the dynamics of classroom environments. In P. Aubusson & S. Schuck, *Teaching, learning and development: The mirror maze*. Dordrecht: Kluwer/Springer.

Johnston, J. M., Anderson, R. R., & DeMeulle, L. (1998). Prospects for collaborative self-study on the internet. In M. L. Hamilton, with S. Pinnegar, T. Russell, J. Loughran, & V. K. LaBoskey (Eds.), *Reconceptualizing teaching practice: Self-study in teacher education,* (pp. 208–223). London: Falmer Press.

Upitis, R., & Russell, T. (1998). Building a teacher education community: Combining electric mail with face-to-face interactions. In M. L. Hamilton, S. Pinnegar, T. Russell, J. Loughran, & V. LaBoskey (Eds.), *Reconceptualizing teaching practice: Self-study in teacher education* (pp. 77–109). London: Falmer Press.

Resource D

Self-Study Related Research Resources

Action Research at Queen's University

According to Action Research at Queen's University, this forum "provides access to a range of materials from action research activities in preservice and graduate programs of the Faculty of Education at Queen's University."

Web site: http://educ.queensu.ca/~ar/

Action Research Net

According to Action Research Net, this forum focuses on "a living educational theory approach to action research, where individuals produce accounts or explanations of their educational influence in their own learning in enquiries of the kind, 'How am I improving what I am doing?' in contexts where they are seeking to live their values more fully in their practice. The living educational theories of pro-

fessional educators usually explain their educational influences in the learning of their students and can also explain educational influences in the learning of social formations."

Web site: http://www.bath.ac.uk/~edsajw/

Center for Instructional Development and Research (CIDR)

According to CIDR, "The Center for Instructional Development and Research recognizes that the University of Washington strives for excellence in three areas: research, teaching, and service. Realizing that members of the UW community have multiple responsibilities within the context of this research-intensive institution, CIDR assists faculty, teaching assistants, departments/units, and administrators with teaching and learning challenges as the UW moves into the 21st Century."

Web site: http://depts.washington.edu/cidrweb/

Council of Great City Schools (CGCS)

According to CGCS, "the Council of the Great City Schools is a coalition of 65 of the nation's largest urban public school systems. It works to promote urban education through legislation, research, media relations, instruction, management, technology, and other special projects designed to improve the quality of urban education. The Council serves as the national voice for urban educators, providing ways to share promising practices and address common concerns."

Web site: http://www.cgcs.org/

Chan, P., & Harris, C. (2002). Enhancement of self-study of teaching practice via creation of video ethnographies.

Society for Information Technology and Teacher Education International Conference 2002(1), 955–957. Chan and Harris state: "Video ethnographies are cases of actual practice in unrehearsed classroom settings. The teachers studied are not actors and neither are their students. There is no effort to sanitize the challenges of teaching nor understate the effort teaching for active learning requires. The complex performances of teaching and learning can be positioned for deep and insightful analysis. When live teaching is observed there is much that goes unnoticed because so many things are happening at once. However, with video ethnographies pre-service and in-service teachers are invited to make multiple observations and interpretations of single episode. The platform for each case is a CD-ROM or

Internet interface which allows pre-service and in-service teachers to explore and build studies of practice."

[Online]. Available: http://dl.aace.org/10961

Education Resources Information Center (ERIC)

According to ERIC, "The Education Resources Information Center (ERIC), sponsored by the Institute of Education Sciences (IES) of the U.S. Department of Education, produces the world's premier database of journal and nonjournal education literature. The ERIC online system provides the public with a centralized ERIC Web site for searching the ERIC bibliographic database of more than 1.1 million citations going back to 1966. More than 107,000 full-text non-journal documents (issued 1993–2004), previously available through fee-based services only, are now available for free. ERIC is moving forward with its modernization program, and has begun adding materials to the database."

Web site: http://www.eric.ed.gov/

Image and Identity Research Collective (IIRC)

According to IIRC, "the collaborators of IIRC share an interest in developing interdisciplinary, image-based research methodologies and artistic forms of representation for the Humanities and Social Sciences. In our individual and collective projects, we variously use video, film, art installations, photography, performance, and fictional practice to research questions relating to gender, age, body, popular culture, and/or identity. Many of our projects involve critical self-study and collective inquiry. In addition to the small group of founding researchers from Concordia and McGill Universities, IIRC's collaborators include faculty and graduate students from other universities as well as independent artists and researchers. Members of the collective use the website to post their work and to "house" bibliographies and other resources that are useful for image-based research. The different kinds of projects which fall within the work of the research collective include:

- The uses of photography in memory work for self-study
- The use of literary forms and live performance to raise critical questions or to represent research and theory
- The exploration of self and identity through artistic installations/productions
- The production and use of documentary/artistic

video for theorizing and reporting research"
Web site: www.iirc.mcgill.ca

Self-Study of Teacher Education Practices Special Interest Group (S-STEP)

According to S-STEP: "We act as a forum for educators who work in a wide variety of settings and who are seeking to make substantial contributions related to the theory and practice of teacher education, self-study research design/practice, and the professional development of teacher educators. We are always very active at the AERA Annual Meetings. The SIG-sponsored social events and annual business meeting give members opportunities to meet one another and discuss issues of self-study design, publishing, ethics, and best practice."

Web site: http://www.ku.edu/~sstep/

S-STEP Community Personal Web Pages

Allan Feldman
Web site: http://www-unix.oit.umass.edu/~afeldman/

Mary Lynn Hamilton
Web site: http://www.people.ku.edu/~hamilton/

Vicki LaBoskey
Web site: http://www.mills.edu/academics/faculty/educ/vickikl/vickikl.php

John J. Loughran
Web site: http://www.education.monash.edu.au/ contacts/staffDetails.php?uid=loughran

Tom Russell
Web site: http://educ.queensu.ca/%7Ear/index.html

Anastasia Samaras
Web site: http://mason.gmu.edu/~asamaras/

Sandra Weber and Claudia Mitchell
Web site: http://www.iirc.mcgill.ca/

Jack Whitehead
Web site: http://www.bath.ac.uk/~edsajw/

The Centre for Arts Informed Research

According to this Web site, "The Centre for Arts-informed Research was established in April 2000. The Centre's mission is to articulate, explore, and support alternative forms of qualitative research and representation which infuse elements, processes, and forms of the arts into scholarly work. Centre Goals: to contribute to the advancement of the genre of arts-informed research; to create a context for emerging and established researchers to explore methodological issues associated with arts-informed research; to work toward the development of a local, national and international community of arts-informed researchers; to promote open dialogue and collaboration among researchers, professional artists, communities, and schools; to provide opportunities and spaces for public access to alternative forms of research."

Web site: http://home.oise.utoronto.ca/~aresearch/airchome3.html/

Teachers for a New Era

According to Teachers for a New Era, it "is a landmark initiative designed to strengthen K-12 teaching by developing state-of-the-art programs at schools of education. With funding from the Carnegie Corporation of New York, the Annenberg Foundation, and the Ford Foundation, this reform initiative has established three guiding principles as critical in the redesign of schools that prepare teachers."

Web site: http://www.teachersforanewera.com

Resource E

AERA and Special Interest Groups

The information listed below about AERA and its affiliated Special Interest Groups is located on the AERA Web site.

American Educational Research Association (AERA)

According to AERA, "The American Educational Research Association founded in 1916, is concerned with improving the educational process by encouraging scholarly inquiry related to education and by promoting the dissemination and practical application of research results. AERA is the most prominent international professional organization with the primary goal of advancing educational research and its practical application. Its 22,000 members are educators; administrators; directors of research; persons working with testing or evaluation in federal, state and local agencies; counselors; evaluators; graduate students; and behavioral

scientists. The broad range of disciplines represented by the membership includes education, psychology, statistics, sociology, history, economics, philosophy, anthropology, and political science."

Web site: http://www.aera.net/

Self-Study Special Interest Group

Self-Study of Teacher Education Practices Special Interest Group (S-STEP) *Purpose:* "To inform and rethink teacher education by studying practice in-varied educational settings and methodologies."

Web site: http://www.ku.edu/~sstep/

Related Special Interest Groups

Action Research

Purpose: "To involve teachers, administrators, researchers, and community members in dialogue about action research that examines educational practice and encourages educational reform and professional development."

Web site: http://explorers.tsuniv.edu/ar-sig/

Arts and Inquiry in the Visual and Performing Arts in Education *(formerly known as International Perspectives on Visual and Performing Arts)*

Purpose: "This international interdisciplinary SIG offers a space for visual artworks, live performance, and theoretical/conceptual praxis, facilitating a platform for artistic researchers and practitioners."

Arts and Learning

Purpose: "Recent themes include arts performance and process in curriculum; arts integration, assessment, and criticism; cultural issues; semiotics creative process; aesthetic education; alternative research methodologies; and constructivism."

Web site: http://www.ed.arizona.edu/ALSIG/

Arts-Based Educational Research

Purpose: "To provide a community for those who view education through artistic lenses, who use a variety of arts-based methodologies, and who communicate understandings through diverse genres."

Critical Issues in Curriculum and Cultural Studies

Purpose: "To support and promote transdisciplinary research of education as experience. The SIG destabilizes commonly held boundaries of educational research beyond contemporary curriculum discourses. Members pursue curriculum inquiry, using critical perspectives, and performative, auto-ethnographic, and conceptual approaches to ask sociocultural, political, and theoretical questions."

Cultural Historical Research

Purpose: "Focuses on human action, agency, and development as mediated by culture, history, and activity in the tradition of Vygotsky, Luria, Leont'ev, Bakhtin, Mead, and others."

Web site: http://ematusov.soe.udel.edu/CH%2DSIG/

Lives of Teachers

Purpose: "To promote discussion and scholarship about teachers, including biography and autobiography, development and dimensions of teachers' careers, and depiction of teachers in fiction, film, and television."

Web site: http://galileo.stmarys-ca.edu/jbrunett/livestch/

Narrative and Research

Purpose: "To support conversations about the place of narratives in educational research, including but not limited to phenomenological, literary, critical, and performative conceptions of narrative analysis."

Web site: http://education.ua.edu/narrativesig/

Teacher as Researcher

Purpose: "To support classroom inquiry research and participation in AERA by PK–12 teachers."

Resource F

The Castle Conferences

The "Castle Conference" or the International Conference of the Self-Study of Teacher Education Practices, provides

an international forum for teacher educators to share examples of self-study in teacher education, to discuss methods and issues in self-study, and to consider the role of self-study in the reform of teacher education.

Web sites: http://educ.queensu.ca/~ar/sstep/

http://www.ku.edu/%7Esstep/castle.htm

Information about the biannual Castle Conferences is listed below:

1996

Richards, J. & Russell, T. (Eds.). (1996). *Empowering our future in teacher education.* Proceedings of the First International Conference on Self-study of Teacher Education Practices, Herstmonceux Castle, East Sussex, England. Kingston, ON: Queen's University.

Web site: http://educ.queensu.ca/~ar/sstep/ S-STEP1–1996.pdf

1998

Cole, A. L., & Finley, S. (Eds.). (1998). *Conversations in community.* Proceedings of the Second International Conference on Self-study of Teacher Education Practices, Herstmonceux Castle, East Sussex, England. Kingston, ON: Queen's University.

Web site: http://educ.queensu.ca/~ar/sstep/ S-STEP2–1998.pdf

2000

Loughran, J., & Russell, T. (Eds.). (2000). *Exploring myths and legends of teacher education.* Proceedings of the Third International Conference on Self-study of Teacher Education Practices, Herstmonceux Castle, East Sussex, England. Kingston, ON: Queen's University.

Web site: http://educ.queensu.ca/~ar/sstep/ S-STEP3–2000.pdf

2002

Kosnik, C., Freese, A., & Samaras, A. P. (Eds.). (2002). *Making a difference in teacher education through self-study.* Proceedings of the Fourth International Conference on Self-study of Teacher Education Practices, Herstmonceux Castle, East Sussex, England (Volumes 1 & 2). Toronto, ON: OISE, University of Toronto.

Web sites: http://educ.queensu.ca/~ar/sstep/

S-STEP4–2002a.pdf

S-STEP4–2002b.pdf

2004

Tidwell, D., Fitzgerald, L., & Heston, M. (Eds.). (2004). *Journeys of hope: Risking the journey of self-study in a diverse world*. Proceedings of the Fifth International Conference on Self-Study of Teacher Education Practices, Herstmonceux Castle, East Sussex, England. Cedar Falls, IA: University of Northern Iowa.

Web site: http://educ.queensu.ca/~ar/sstep/ S-STEP5–2004.pdf

2006

10th Anniversary Castle Conference

Fitzgerald, L., Heston, M., & Tidwell, D. (Eds.). (2006). *Collaboration and community: Pushing boundaries through self-study*. Proceedings of the Sixth International Conference on Self-Study of Teacher Education Practices, Herstmonceux Castle, East Sussex, England. Cedar Falls, IA: University of Northern Iowa.

Web site: http://educ.queensu.ca/~ar/sstep/ S-STEP6–2006.pdf

Resource G

Related Conferences

Arts-based Educational Research Conference

http://www.qub.ac.uk/edu/news_and_events/ABER_brochure.pdf

The Ontario Institute for Studies in Education of the University of Toronto, Toronto, Canada. An international conference on initial teacher education and the subsequent first years of a teacher's career

Web site: http://conference.oise.utoronto.ca/

East Side Institute for Group and Short Term Psychotherapy

According to the Web page, "The East Side Institute for Group and Short Term Psychotherapy is an international training and research center for new approaches to human development and community building. Since the mid-1970s, we have worked to change psychology from a diagnostic, evaluative (and often stigmatizing) social science into a positive and creative force for the emotional, social and cultural development of all people and their communities."

Web site: http://www.eastsideinstitute.org/

Resource H

Additional Invitations to Practice

In Chapter 4, we shared three invitations to practice relating to the purposes of personal, professional, and classroom/schoolwide improvement. Within that frame, we offered invitations using various self-study methods, i.e., first, a personal history self-study method, second, a developmental portfolio self-study method, and, third, an arts-based self-study method incorporating visual representations. Below we share additional invitations to practice which will introduce you to further methods of self-study. You can shape your focus and purpose for your exploration in this improvement-aimed work. Enjoy experimenting with these self-study methods:

- Memory Work Self-Study Method
- Collective Self-Study Method
- Arts-Based Self-Study Method—Portraits
- Arts-Based Self-Study Method—Improvisation
- Arts-Based Self-Study Method—Performance
- Arts-Based Self-Study Method—Photography

Invitation to Practice
Memory Work Self-Study Method

A Retrospective Journey

(Adapted from the work of Mitchell & Weber, 1999. Also see Allender, 2001, and Allender & Manke, 2004).

Purpose

Memory work is a self-study method used to represent autobiographical inquiry with critical and reflective revisiting. Memory serves to "uncover the ways in which individuals build their identities . . . what we remember and how we remember the events in our lives to form the basis of whom [sic] and what we are today" (O'Reilly-Scanlon, 2002, p. 74). Memory work makes the past usable and helps inform your professional future (Weber & Mitchell, 2002).

Context

(You add your own personal context.)

Wonderings/questions

- How can examining, discussing, and inquiring about my past inform my teaching?
- What role can artifacts play in that process?
- How is my personal and professional growth enriched through conversations and critique with colleagues?

Process and Data Collection

1 Invite a trusted colleague to participate in this activity with you.

2 Collect artifacts or objects from your past that say something about you as a learner, e.g., diaries, CDs, photos, books, postcards, reports, videos, hobby projects, club and school memorabilia, uniforms, t-shirts, or other items that recall a memory of your learning past. Memory work can incorporate written and/or art forms, e.g., journaling, diaries, poetry, photographs, art installations, and videos. You read about the diaries that Mitchell (2005) used in the Chapter 4. It can also include artifacts that you have collected from your past.

3 Examine your group of artifacts. Choose one artifact that especially stands out for you.
- Write your story behind the artifact. This is your first draft. Here are some suggested prompts:
- Why did you choose this artifact?
- Describe the social context and the historical period. What is the setting?
- Who are the characters in your story?
- What is the conflict or scene?
- What role does your artifact play in the story?
- What part do you play in the story?

Collaboration

4 Pair Share Session
- Read your draft to your colleague. Listen carefully to your story as you retell it.
- Listen to each other tell about the memory related to the particular artifact.
- Take notes on what you hear from each other's stories.
- Then reflect and discuss why you might

have remembered this story and why you
remembered it in the way you did.

- Discuss how your story relates to your work
  as a teacher.
- Share your notes.

5   Now rewrite your story with a more honest
    stance. Consider what wasn't actually true or
    maybe something you wrote that was a stretch
    of the truth. Mitchell and Weber (1999) suggest
    writing this second draft in the third person
    which makes it possible to 'step outside' one's self.

6   Share your revised story with your colleague.

Sustaining, Concluding, Extending Activities

7   You might also reflect on any connections between
    particular artifacts. Do they belong to a partic-
    ular historical period of your learning past?
    Experiment with placing and pairing artifacts
    in a second story and repeat the process.

Group Work

8   Find other colleagues and repeat the experience.
    You may decide to choose a different artifact
    and talk about that object. Revisit the prompts
    above and add your own.

9   Talk about any differences you note in this
    extended circle of conversation.

Evidence of Impact

- What were the differences between your first
  and second draft?
- What is the role of artifact and story in your
  teaching life?
- Are there implications of this memory work to
  your classroom and students?
- How might you adapt this activity to your
  teaching?

Invitation to Practice
Collective Self-Study Method

Collaboration in a Virtual Setting

(Adapted from the work of Kosnik, Samaras, & Freese, 2006)

Purpose

The collective self-study method involves a group of people who collaboratively design, implement, and evaluate a self-study project. The collaboration involves an ongoing dialogue among the teachers for the purpose of personal, professional, classroom, and/or program development. The context can be in a face-to-face context, a virtual context, or a combination of those. Teachers respond to each other constantly, consistently, and over time. One self-study project might be an exploration about the dynamics of their team work in a virtual setting and the implications of that work to their teaching and programs.

Context

(You add your own personal context.)

Wonderings/questions

- How effective have I been working in a collaborative virtual setting?
- What factors do I think contribute to our group's success and to our difficulties?
- In what ways can my work with this group facilitate my understanding of team work in my home institution?

Process and Data Collection

1 Collect and store your e-mail interactions and any other electronic correspondence such as attachment files, faxes, videos, CDs. Also store notes of your phone or video-conferencing sessions and any mailed correspondence.

2 Identify your questions, i.e., what would you like to study about your practices together in this virtual setting?

3 Begin to read through your data. Sort, analyze, and interpret the data individually at this point. The analysis includes a content analysis of your e-mail correspondence.

4 You might consider the paradoxes presented in Chapter 3 of this book. Self-study is, first of all, individual and collective, second, personal and interpersonal; and, third, private and public. Do your data support any of these paradoxes?

Collaboration

5   Hold several conference call sessions, and if possible, some face-to-face interactions to discuss your thinking, questions, new insights, and interpretations.

6   Share your insights and interpretations and compare your findings to that of your colleagues. Discuss the evidence you each found. Compare, combine, and negotiate the categories you each found.

Here are some possible probing questions that could move your dialogue and analysis along. You might ask questions such as:

- What have I learned about being a team member?
- What do I believe is my greatest contribution to this team?
- What areas need further development in my role as a virtual team member?
- How has this team supported and valued my work?
- How have I supported and valued their work?
- What specific challenges have I faced in this teaming experience?
- How has my team helped me question who I am as a teacher?
- What are some things that stand out for me in this experience in terms of my professional growth?
- What would I say has changed the most for me over time? How do I know that?
- What do I believe contributes to our effectiveness as a team?
- What areas do I believe need further work?
- In what ways if any have I transferred my new learnings to other collaborative experiences?

Sustaining, Concluding, Extending Activities

7   Present your work to other virtual teams and organizations and seek their feedback.

Evidence of Impact

- What have you learned about the nature of your virtual learning community?
- What were the strengths and limitations of your work in this context?

- What evidence can you provide to document your findings?

Invitation to Practice
Arts-Based Self-Study Method—Portraits

Reading a Self-Portrait

(Adapted from the work of Weber & Mitchell, 1996, 2004. Also see Richards, 1998).

Purpose

Self-portraits are a form of text useful for reading, broadening, and communicating an understanding of one's teaching practice, students, learning contexts, and structures of schooling. Self-portraits generate data useful for teachers' professional knowing. Dialogue with peers about teaching portraits is a means to construct and reconstruct your thinking about who you are as a teacher.

Context

(You add your own personal context.)

Wonderings/questions

- How do I see myself as a teacher?
- What do I want to change in my teaching and classroom? How might I go about that change?
- What role can peers play in the reframing process?

Process and Data Collection

1   Draw or make a self-portrait of how you see yourself as a teacher. Choose your medium and materials, e.g., sketch paper, pencils, poster paper, markers, clay, crepe paper, felt, colored pencils, oil paint, watercolor sets, crayons, cardboard, wood, etc. This activity does not require any artistic training in portrait making.

2   After you complete your self-portrait, step back and examine it carefully.

3   Then, reflect and write about your portrait. Include your thoughts and reactions to what you have drawn. Ask questions that come to mind as you critically examine your portrait. Here are some ideas:

- How does this self-portrait relate to my learning and teaching experiences?
- Does the self-portrait showcase any particular learning or teaching dilemma?
- Is this portrait related to any recent interaction in my teaching?
- What does it portray about my perception of my identity and gender as a teacher? Notice your clothes, props, physical features, expression, etc.
- Do I notice any stereotypes about teachers that I portrayed? Interpret any popular notions of teachers you portrayed.
- When and where does it take place? Pay attention to the historical, social, and cultural context of your self-portrait.
- Is anyone else included in my self-portrait? Are there students in the drawing?
- Is there anyone in the portrait background? If so, what does it suggest about my relationship to those persons?
- Are there objects in my self-portrait? Do they carry any special meaning to me and/or to my students?
- What would I title this portrait?

Collaboration

4 Pair Share Session
- After you complete your self-portrait, ask a colleague to react to your portrait without judgment.
- Your colleague might also decide to make his/her self-portrait.
- Talk about what you are learning about each other.
- Share your hopes for yourself as a teacher.
- What do you wish was different?
- What are your projected professional goals?
- What resources will you need?
- How will you go about achieving this goal?

5 Re-Portraiting
- Now draw a new portrait that depicts a renewed vision of you as a teacher.

Sustaining, Concluding, Extending Activities

6 Group Work
- You may choose to extend this activity with

a group of colleagues. If so, find somewhere where your can comfortably gather and spread out your self-portraits.

- What is your reaction to these images? How do others react to them?
- Hold a conversation about what you see in the group of self-portraits.
- Observe and comment on any commonalities and differences that emerge when comparing the two sets of portraits on an individual level and then collectively.
- Synthesize how you and your colleagues view teachers overall.
- What are the challenges and hopes of teachers as portrayed through the portraits?

Evidence of Impact

- What awareness has this activity raised for you about who you think you are as a teacher?
- Reflect and document any differences you experience in your teaching and any changes in your students' learning after you conduct this activity.

Invitation to Practice
Arts-Based Self-Study Method—Improvisation

Differences through Drama

(Adapted from the work of Samaras with Reed, 2000)

Purpose

One way to begin to think about students' individual differences in your classroom is to consider the difficulties you observe and how you deal with them. Performance is a method of seeing those differences. It is a way of seeing others and ourselves more clearly. Improvisation promotes perspective-taking and sharing alternative points of view about those differences.

Context

(You add your own personal context.)

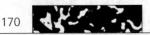

Wonderings/questions

- How do I see my students' individual differences?
- What impact do those individual differences have on my teaching?
- How can I acknowledge the individual differences in learning for myself and for my students?

Process and Data Collection

1   Begin by reflecting on the individual differences in your own learning from that of your peers. Invite a peer to also participate in this activity.

2   Write a short narrative about your differences. Consider:
- In what ways do you remember your learning as different from those around you?
- Were those differences an advantage or disadvantage for you?
- How were those differences supported or not supported in your schooling?

3   Next, write a narrative on student individual differences in learning you have observed in your classroom. Include your actions and reactions toward those differences.

4   Read through the two sets of narratives and circle any commonalities or patterns.

Collaboration

Pair Share Session

5   Read your narrative about your difference and the one about your students' differences to your colleague. Take turns.

6   Join two other colleagues and listen to their narratives.

7   Next, the group selects a narrative to perform to another group.

8   The group enacts the narrative in an improvisation to the other group.

9   Colleagues can freeze a frame of the improvisation at any point and intervene to extend the improvisation.

10   Gather collegial ideas through stepping inside and outside of different roles and scenes and through colleagues' extensions of the narrative.

11   Discuss what you perceive as the conflict, change, or dilemma in the improvisation. Is it resolved? How?

Sustaining, Concluding, Extending Activities

12   Repeat the process with other narratives.

Evidence of Impact

- Hold a discussion about the experience. What are you more conscious about in terms of your learning differences and that of your students?
- How might you use this activity in your classroom?

Invitation to Practice

Arts-Based Self-Study Method—Performance

Be the Teacher

(Adapted from the work of Samaras with Reed, 2000. Also see Ben-Peretz, 1995, and Weber & Mitchell, 2004)

Purpose

Performance is a method of documenting the emotional side of teaching and the self-study of that with others. Performance is a method of seeing others and ourselves more clearly. Enacting the challenges and difficulties of teaching can be important professional learning tools.

Context

(You add your own personal context.)

Wonderings/questions

- What do I consider the most satisfying factors in my teaching life?
- What do I think I can learn from seasoned teachers?
- How does performance help me understand teaching?

Process and Data Collection

1   Ask a seasoned teacher to share a story about his/her teaching with you.
2   Request that the story be about something that carried strong emotional responses for them. The prompt question for the interview is for the person to talk about, describe, or explain something in their past teaching that they found

exceptionally moving, joyful, wounding, or both. It should be a story they are willing to share and have others hear about although their names will not be revealed. Be sure to gain permission to share and perform his/her story.

3 Find a quiet place. Try to just listen carefully and patiently to the teacher's story. If your interviewee wants to tell you more, listen and observe. This should be a wonderful time for both of you.

4 Keep notes on the verbal and non-verbal conversation. This becomes your script.

5 After the interview, choose and share a segment of the interview that you will present to your colleagues through a performance.

6 Rehearse it in the character of the teacher you interviewed, using his/her voice, vocal pattern, stance, gestures, and appearance. Completely give yourself to that person. Be prepared to perform "as if" you were that person you interviewed as much as possible. The performance should not last longer than 5 minutes.

Collaboration

7 Hold a discussion about what you learned by performing someone else. If your colleagues also participated in this activity, you might choose to take turns in a 'Talk Host' format with colleagues to capture what you learned from your colleagues' performances. One of you can play the talk host and the other can share what they learned. Here are some prompts for your discussion:

- What did the seasoned teachers seem to remember most?
- Were there any themes/categories of topics, successes, challenges that were recalled?
- Was there any grand theme in the content of the interviews?
- Did age or discipline appear to be a factor in their stories?
- What appears to be the most satisfying factors in teachers' lives?
- How did they overcome difficulties?
- What professional wisdom do these retired teachers offer us?

Sustaining, Concluding, Extending Activities

8   Tell a story of your teaching and have a colleague enact it.

Evidence of Impact

- What data emerged from your performance and discussion?
- What did you learn from observing your colleagues' performances?
- Write about this experience for you and compare your conclusions with that of your colleagues.

Invitation to Practice

Arts-Based Self-Study Method—Photography

Visual Literacy through Multiple Lenses

(Adapted from the work of Mitchell & Weber, 1998, 2004).

Purpose

Photography promotes reflection and dialogue and captures a moment in time of teaching. Visual images are transitions for thought and expression. Photography is a way of knowing that creates a distance and exchange of perspectives about the teacher self.

Context

(You add your own personal context.)

Wonderings/questions

- What can photographs teach me about my teaching?
- Do I see myself with the same lens as others see me?
- How can a camera be a research tool?

Process and Data Collection

1   Choose a colleague to participate with you in this activity.

2   Write three adjectives that best describe you as a teacher. Reflect and inquire, "How do I see myself?" "How would I describe myself as a teacher?" "How do I think my students see me?"

3 Share your adjectives and reflections with each other.

4 Prepare to take a photograph of yourself as a teacher. Be sure to obtain informed consent of anyone else in the photograph, e.g., students, other teachers, parents, etc.

5 Get your camera equipment ready and bring it to your classroom. Decide on the context, background, size, length, color, composition, distance, and angle of the photo. Play with the zoom lens. Set your camera on a tripod with a timer.

6 Take a picture of yourself or frame the photograph and ask someone else to take it. Consider how the photograph can best depict you as teacher.

7 Afterwards, look at your photograph and adjectives.

8 How does your interpretation of your photograph align or misalign with your adjectives?

Collaboration

Pair Share Session

9 Share your interpretation of your photograph and adjectives with a colleague. Discuss your interpretations.

Sustaining, Concluding, and Extending Activities

10 Ask your colleague to take several rolls of candid shots of you teaching. You can decide if the photographs are taken from one day or many days and over a designated time period. You can also decide if the photographs are taken in a particular class or in many classes. Digital cameras give immediate results and can be shared easily with others.

11 Next, look at the photographs your colleague took.

12 Engage in a critical dialogue with your colleague about this activity and the emotions it stirs for you. Actively listen. Here are some ideas:

- Title selective photographs that show a similar pattern.
- Tell a story about one of the photographs.
- What do the photographs say about you as a teacher?
- What surprised you?

- Notice the background, objects, shapes, subject, and the layout of the photograph.
- Are there other people in the photograph? Where are they in relation to you?
- Focus in on your expression and stance.
- How are the photographs the same and/or different?
- Are there any themes that emerge as you examine the photographs as data?
- Repeat the process with your colleague now with his/her photographs.
- Share your photos with students, colleagues, and parents.
- Repeat this activity at a later time and compare your findings.
- You may also decide to create a photograph that depicts you in the future.
- Change the context of the photograph to a place outside the classroom; a place where you learn, play, live, etc.
- Continue to experiment with photography and your teaching through the medium of collage making or videotaping. (See Mitchell & Weber, 1999, and Weber & Mitchell, 2004 for suggestions on using videotaping.)

Evidence of Impact

- What have you learned about your teaching through photography?
- What have you learned through the feedback of your colleague?
- How have you used photographs as data?

Peter Lang PRIMERS

in Education

Peter Lang Primers are designed to provide a brief and concise introduction or supplement to specific topics in education. Although sophisticated in content, these primers are written in an accessible style, making them perfect for undergraduate and graduate classroom use. Each volume includes a glossary of key terms and a References and Resources section.

Other published and forthcoming volumes cover such topics as:

- Standards
- Popular Culture
- Critical Pedagogy
- Literacy
- Higher Education
- John Dewey
- Feminist Theory and Education

- Studying Urban Youth Culture
- Multiculturalism through Postformalism
- Creative Problem Solving
- Teaching the Holocaust
- Piaget and Education
- Deleuze and Education
- Foucault and Education

Look for more Peter Lang Primers to be published soon. To order other volumes, please contact our Customer Service Department:

> 800-770-LANG (within the US)
> 212-647-7706 (outside the US)
> 212-647-7707 (fax)

To find out more about this and other Peter Lang book series, or to browse a full list of education titles, please visit our website:

> **www.peterlang.com**